James Joyce's

A PORTRAIT
OF THE ARTIST
AS A YOUNG MAN

The Adventures of Huckleberry Finn
Mark Twain

Aeneid
Vergil

Animal Farm
George Orwell

The Autobiography of Malcolm X
Alex Haley & Malcolm X

Beowulf

**Billy Budd, Benito Cereno,
& Bartleby the Scrivener**
Herman Melville

Brave New World
Aldous Huxley

The Catcher in the Rye
J. D. Salinger

Crime and Punishment
Fyodor Dostoevsky

The Crucible
Arthur Miller

Death of a Salesman
Arthur Miller

The Divine Comedy (Inferno)
Dante

A Farewell to Arms
Ernest Hemingway

Frankenstein
Mary Shelley

The Grapes of Wrath
John Steinbeck

Great Expectations
Charles Dickens

The Great Gatsby
F. Scott Fitzgerald

Gulliver's Travels
Jonathan Swift

Hamlet
William Shakespeare

Heart of Darkness & The Secret Sharer
Joseph Conrad

Henry IV, Part One
William Shakespeare

I Know Why the Caged Bird Sings
Maya Angelou

Iliad
Homer

Invisible Man
Ralph Ellison

Jane Eyre
Charlotte Brontë

Julius Caesar
William Shakespeare

King Lear
William Shakespeare

Lord of the Flies
William Golding

Macbeth
William Shakespeare

A Midsummer Night's Dream
William Shakespeare

Moby-Dick
Herman Melville

Native Son
Richard Wright

Nineteen Eighty-Four
George Orwell

Odyssey
Homer

Oedipus Plays
Sophocles

Of Mice and Men
John Steinbeck

The Old Man and the Sea
Ernest Hemingway

Othello
William Shakespeare

Paradise Lost
John Milton

Pride and Prejudice
Jane Austen

The Red Badge of Courage
Stephen Crane

Romeo and Juliet
William Shakespeare

The Scarlet Letter
Nathaniel Hawthorne

Silas Marner
George Eliot

The Sun Also Rises
Ernest Hemingway

A Tale of Two Cities
Charles Dickens

Tess of the D'Urbervilles
Thomas Hardy

To Kill a Mockingbird
Harper Lee

Uncle Tom's Cabin
Harriet Beecher Stowe

Wuthering Heights
Emily Brontë

James Joyce's
A PORTRAIT
OF THE ARTIST
AS A YOUNG MAN

Bloom's NOTES

A CONTEMPORARY
LITERARY VIEWS BOOK

Edited and with an Introduction by
HAROLD BLOOM

First Printing
1 3 5 7 9 8 6 4 2

Library of Congress Cataloging-in-Publication Data

The hardback of this edition has been cataloged as follows:

James Joyce's A portrait of the artist as a young man / edited and with an introduction by Harold Bloom.
p. 82   cm. — (Bloom's notes)
Includes bibliographical references and index.
ISBN 0-7910-4570-6(hc) 0-7910-4566-8 (pb)
1. Joyce, James, 1882-1941. Portrait of the artist as a young man—
Examinations—Study guides.   2. Dublin (Ireland)—In literature—
Examinations—Study guides.   3. Young men in literature—
—Examinations—Study guides.   I. Bloom, Harold.   II. Series.
PR6019.O9P6455   1998
823'.912—dc21
98-16607
CIP

Chelsea House Publishers
1974 Sproul Road, Suite 400
Broomall, PA 19008-0914

Contents

User's Guide

This volume is designed to present biographical, critical, and bibliographical information on the author and the work. Following Harold Bloom's editor's note and introduction are a detailed biography of the author, discussing major life events and important literary works. Then follows a thematic and structural analysis of the work, which traces significant themes, patterns, and motifs. An annotated list of characters supplies brief information on the chief characters in the work.

A selection of critical extracts, derived from previously published material by leading critics, then follows. The extracts consist of statements by the author, early reviews of the work, and later evaluations up to the present. These items are arranged chronologically by date of first publication. A bibliography of the author's writings (including a complete list of all books written, cowritten, edited, and translated), a list of additional books and articles on the author and the work, and an index of themes conclude the volume.

Harold Bloom is Sterling Professor of the Humanities at Yale University and Henry W. and Albert A. Berg Professor of English at the New York University Graduate School. He is the author of twenty books and the editor of more than thirty anthologies of literary criticism.

Professor Bloom's works include *Shelley's Mythmaking* (1959), *The Visionary Company* (1961), *Blake's Apocalypse* (1963), *Yeats* (1970), *A Map of Misreading* (1975), *Kabbalah and Criticism* (1975), and *Agon: Towards a Theory of Revisionism* (1982). *The Anxiety of Influence* (1973) sets forth Professor Bloom's provocative theory of the literary relationships between the great writers and their predecessors. His most recent books include *The American Religion* (1992), *The Western Canon* (1994), and *Omens of Millennium: The Gnosis of Angels, Dreams, and Resurrection* (1996).

Professor Bloom earned his Ph.D. from Yale University in 1955 and has served on the Yale faculty since then. He is a 1985 MacArthur Foundation Award recipient and served as the Charles Elkot Norton Professor of Poetry at Harvard University in 1987–88. He is currently the editor of other Chelsea House series in literary criticism, including MAJOR LITERARY CHARACTERS, MODERN CRITICAL VIEWS, and WOMEN WRITERS OF ENGLISH AND THEIR WORKS.

Editor's Note

My Introduction meditates upon the aestheticism of Stephen Dedalus, finding in it Joyce's own essential stance as a writer.

The Critical Extracts commence with Edward Garnett's "Reader's Report" upon the manuscript of the *Portrait*, asking for more revisions. H. G. Wells praises the novel for its Swiftian qualities, while Ezra Pound invokes Flaubert as an analogue, and John C. Squire commends Joyce's realism.

Herbert S. Gorman sees the *Portrait* as authentic autobiography, after which Harry Levin emphasizes Joyce's impressionism as a prose artist. The Irish-American novelist James T. Farrell examines the theme of exile from Ireland, while Hugh Kenner centers upon the novel's opening.

Joyce's great biographer, Richard Ellmann, relates Joyce's exile to the book's vision of aesthetic freedom, after which the exuberant Joycean novelist, Anthony Burgess explores the metaphor of flight in the *Portrait*.

Evert Sprinchorn, in the mode of Kenner, finds Stephen insufferable unless interpreted esoterically, while A. Walton Litz analyzes symbolic structures in the novel. Stephen's struggle against his infatuation with Emma is viewed by C. H. Peake as crucial to the process of becoming an artist.

The images of hands in the *Portrait* are unified by James Carens, after which Martin Price powerfully expounds Stephen's sense of the relationship between an artist and his art.

Patrick Parrinder traces Stephen's credo of art as salvation to the influence of Wordsworth and Shelley, while Joseph A. Buttigieg emphasizes instead the historical obstacles to Stephen's quest.

For John Blades, the Joycean epiphany is a mode of revealing truth, which fits Patrick Colm Hogan's comparison of Joyce to another great prophet of truth, John Milton.

In a final extract, David Glover shrewdly relates Joyce's general fame to some of the ways in which high culture and popular culture have merged.

Introduction

HAROLD BLOOM

James Joyce was a lapsed Irish Catholic, educated by the Jesuits, but firmly opposed to the Church on matters of faith, morals, politics, and the autonomy of imaginative literature. This did not save Joyce's writings from being baptized by T. S. Eliot, who found Joyce to be "eminently orthodox." The critic Hugh Kenner followed in Eliot's wake and deprecated the Stephen Dedalus of *A Portrait of the Artist as a Young Man*. Joyce's self-portrait as a young man, according to Kenner, was wholly ironic. Dedalus is an aesthete in the mode of Walter Pater and Oscar Wilde: "Every portrait that is painted with feeling is a portrait of the artist," according to Wilde. To Kenner, Joyce's Stephen is "indigestibly Byronic." The great critic William Empson denounced this as "the Kenner Smear," and defended Stephen's aestheticism as being essentially Joyce's own, as clearly it is. Stephen is reborn as an artist well before he achieves anything as a writer. His aestheticism is a secular faith, informed by Ibsen and Shelley as well as by Pater, and always remained Joyce's credo.

Joyce's early intellectual vision centered upon what he called "epiphanies," privileged moments of perception, flashes of radiance against a darkening background. In *Stephen Hero*, the earlier version of what became the *Portrait*, the epiphany is defined by Stephen as

> . . . a sudden spiritual manifestation . . . He believed that it was for the man of letters to record these epiphanies with extreme care, seeing that they themselves are the most delicate and evanescent of moments.

Walter Pater is the precursor here, with his mode of criticism founded upon the perception of privileged moments of vision, and the sensation of the brevity and intensity of those epiphanies. Like Joyce, Pater asked these epiphanies for very little, really only for a certain longing, as here in *The Renaissance*:

A sudden light transfigures a trivial thing, a weathervane, a windmill, a winnowing flail, the dust in the barn door; a moment—and the thing has vanished, because it was pure effect; but it leaves a relish behind it, a longing that the accident may happen again.

The great epiphany in the *Portrait* comes just before the novel's conclusion:

The spell of arms and voices: the white arms of roads, their promise of close embraces and the black arms of tall ships that stand against the moon, their tale of distant nations. They are held out to say: We are alone. Come. And the voices say with them: We are your kinsmen. And the air is thick with their company as they call to me, their kinsman, making ready to go, shaking the wings of their exultant and terrible youth.

A High Romantic rhapsody, and not an ironic distancing, this has an aura of belatedness that mingles with its triumphalism. The visionary company of love calls out to Stephen, who goes into exile in order to join the writers who preceded him in that region of unlikeness. An even more intense cognitive music is evoked in Stephen's most famous declamation:

Welcome, O life! I go to encounter for the millionth time the reality of experience and to forge in the smithy of my soul the uncreated conscience of my race.

To forge here is to perform the work of Blake's Los, the blacksmith of Eternity, and also of Ibsen's Brand, who said he possessed the fire to transform "the uncreated soul of man." More than 80 years after its creation, *A Portrait of the Artist as a Young Man* has become a permanent work of the imagination. Stephen Dedalus remains a universal emblem for the struggle to become an artist. He is not Joyce's ironic dismissal of an earlier Romantic self, but rather a heroic incarnation of the poetic character. Stephen goes into an exile as fecund as Dante's, because out of it will come *Ulysses* and *Finnegans Wake*. ❖

Biography of
James Joyce

(1882–1941)

James Augustine Aloysius Joyce was born on the outskirts of Dublin on February 2, 1882, to John Stanislaus Joyce, a civil servant, and Mary Jane Murray Joyce. Unlike his alter ego, the grim Stephen Dedalus, Joyce was a relatively happy child who earned the nickname "Sunny Jim" from his parents. The oldest of ten children, Joyce remained close only to his brother Stanislaus (b. 1884), who would be the only member of the family to read his brother's work.

Joyce received a thorough education in Catholic and scholastic doctrine beginning at Clongowes Wood College; when his chronically insolvent father could no longer afford the school's fees he transferred to Dublin's Belvedere College. From 1898 to 1902 Joyce attended University College in Dublin. Though he distinguished himself academically, learning French, Italian, German, Norwegian, and Latin, he distanced himself from religion and from nationalist literary and political movements. When he was 18 he published a review of Ibsen's *When We Dead Awaken* in the *Fortnightly Review*, which received a complimentary response from the author. In the same year Joyce also wrote a play, *A Brilliant Career*, which he later destroyed.

In 1902, dissatisfied and disillusioned with Irish nationalism, Catholicism, and his family background, Joyce left Ireland to spend the rest of his life in exile in Paris, Trieste, Rome, and Zürich; he would visit Ireland only occasionally. Joyce went first to Paris to study medicine, supporting himself by teaching English; he returned to Dublin in 1904, however, to be with his dying mother. During this time, Joyce began work on an autobiographical first novel and on several short stories.

On June 16 of that year (the same day on which the action of *Ulysses* takes place), Joyce met a Galway woman named Nora

Barnacle; she returned to Europe with him in 1904. They had two children, Giorgio (b. 1905) and Lucia Anna (b. 1907), but did not marry until the death of Joyce's father in 1931 compelled them to do so to protect their children's legal rights. For several years, the Joyces wandered through Europe, settling first in Trieste in 1905, where Joyce taught at the Berlitz School of Languages. At the start of the First World War he was under "free arrest" in Austria; he and his family were permitted to move to Zürich in 1915.

In Ireland, Joyce had published a collection of poems entitled *Chamber Music* (1907), as well as several short stories. After a nine-year battle with publishers and printers, the short story collection *Dubliners* appeared in 1914. Under the editorship of Ezra Pound, *A Portrait of the Artist as a Young Man* was published in serial form in *The Egoist* from 1914 to 1915; it appeared in book form in 1916.

Joyce's financial difficulties were eased somewhat in 1916 by a Civil List grant and by the support of Harriet Shaw Weaver, editor of *The Egoist* (until his last years, he earned almost nothing from his publications). In Zürich he organized a company of Irish actors, who gave the first performance of his play *Exiles* (1918).

Joyce had begun writing *Ulysses* in 1914. From 1918 to 1920 the novel was published serially in *The Little Review* in New York, but publication was halted in 1920 because of an obscenity suit brought against Joyce. The court scandal only enhanced the author's reputation. On February 2, 1922—Joyce's 40th birthday—*Ulysses* was published in book form by The Egoist Press of England and Shakespeare and Co. of Paris, but it remained banned in England and America. Though the ban improved sales, *Ulysses* also earned critical praise as a major work of literature. After additional legal battles, the book was declared fit for publication and released in the United States in 1934 by Random House—upon Judge Woolsley's famous declaration that the book is "emetic" rather than "an aphrodisiac"—and in England in 1936.

Beginning in 1922, Joyce began work on another novel, sections of which appeared in various forms over the next 16 years as *Work in Progress*; it appeared complete in 1939 as *Finnegans Wake*, Joyce's most complex and elusive work. During this period, Joyce's personal life grew increasingly difficult. He had always suffered from weak eyesight; between 1917 and 1930 he underwent 11 eye operations. In 1932 his beloved daughter, Lucia, was diagnosed with schizophrenia; she was institutionalized the following year.

With the outbreak of World War II, Joyce was again forced to flee to Zürich. His fame and prosperity had greatly increased by this time; but he had become nearly blind, forced to depend on his memory and secretarial help to continue working. He died in Zürich on January 13, 1941. ❖

Thematic and Structural Analysis

In 1906, ten years before the publication of *A Portrait of the Artist as a Young Man*, James Joyce wrote about his plan to publish an autobiographical novel. He envisioned a book that would describe the emotional high points of his life and chart his growth toward maturity. Rather than being historically comprehensive, he explained, the book would depict those high points as vividly as possible in terms of what Joyce later called "epiphanies," or moments of heightened spiritual and intellectual awareness. *A Portrait of the Artist* represents those experiences from the perspective of the Joycelike protagonist, Stephen Dedalus.

Stephen's last name and the novel's Latin epigraph from *Ovid's Metamorphoses*, "*Et ignotas animum dimittit in artes*" ("And he applied his mind to obscure arts"), refer to Daedalus, an Athenian artist and inventor in Greek mythology. Imprisoned in a labyrinth by the Cretan King Minos, Daedalus (whose name means "cunning artificer") constructs two pairs of wings fastened with wax so that he and his son, Icarus, can escape. Delighted by his ability to fly, Icarus soars too close to the sun; the wax melts and he plunges into the sea and drowns. Daedalus, however, arrives safely in Sicily. Father and son in this tale are often interpreted as representing the classical artist and the romantic artist, respectively. Throughout the novel, Joyce employs images of artistry, flight, and escape to represent Stephen's struggle to emerge from his past and become a truly autonomous artist.

In the opening section of **chapter one**, Stephen's early childhood is presented as a series of sensory images simulating a child's first impressions. Although these images are distilled into seemingly random linguistic fragments, this section is intricately structured. Many of the thematic elements introduced in the first two pages will resurface in expanded form throughout the novel.

In the first six paragraphs of the book, all of three-year-old Stephen's physical senses—sight (his father's face), hearing (the nursery tale and song), touch (the wet sheets on the bed), taste (the lemon platt), and smell (the oilsheet and his parents)—are stimulated. Stephen's understanding of himself as a physical being is based on these earliest and most lasting memories: "When you wet the bed first it is warm then it gets cold," the child observes. "His mother put on the oilsheet. That had the queer smell." Such shifts between warm and cold sensations, for example, will become linked in the older Stephen's mind to thoughts of sex and religion, pleasure and guilt, the physical and the spiritual. In the same way, Joyce uses imagery of wetness and dryness to connote nature (or sinfulness) versus learning (or virtue), and light and darkness to imply knowledge (or reason) and ignorance (or irrationality).

Joyce also employs colors throughout *A Portrait of the Artist* as symbols of opposing values or forces. While still a toddler, Stephen learns about the colors of political affiliations: the two clothes brushes of Dante Riordan, his governess, are backed with maroon velvet—for Michael Davitt, an early ally of Charles Stewart Parnell, and green velvet—for Parnell himself, an Irish Nationalist regarded as a hero by advocates of Irish independence. When Parnell becomes involved in an adultery and divorce scandal, Dante rips the green velvet back off the brush and tells Stephen that "Parnell was a bad man." Likewise, the colors red and yellow symbolize courage and cowardice or health and sickness in the novel's later chapters.

A Portrait of the Artist opens as Simon Dedalus, Stephen's father, is telling a nursery tale about a "moocow" as he peers down at his child. This fragmented memory leads to another of the boy singing his favorite song about a wild rose (H. S. Thompson's song "Lily Dale," which describes the death of a child), and a harsh nursery song adapted from a book by Isaac Watts, an eighteenth-century English theologian and hymn writer. This chant, "Pull out his eyes,/Apologise," ends the first section by anticipating the severe punishments that Stephen will endure during his attendance at Clongowes Wood College, the Jesuit boarding school where Joyce began his own studies.

Stephen's next memory is of Clongowes. He is about six years old and is competing with a group of boisterous schoolmates in a game of football (rugby). A small, weak child with poor vision, Stephen feels lost amid the "whirl of scrimmage," afraid of the "flashing eyes and muddy boots" around him. Intensely homesick, he thinks about the day that his parents left him at Clongowes and counts the days until he will return home for the holidays. He reflects that he would rather be indoors, in the study hall or lying before a fireplace and reading "nice sentences in Doctor Cornwell's Spelling Book."

This "warm" thought brings Stephen to recall with a shiver the day he was pushed into the square ditch (a cesspool behind the dormitory) by a bullying schoolmate named Wells. The vivid description of the "cold slimy water." against his skin is followed by a comforting scene of home—Dante, with her feet propped before the fire—and of the pleasures of scholarship ("Dante was a clever woman and a well read woman").

Stephen develops a fever as a result of his fall into the cesspool. As the fever worsens, he remembers events and scenes in terms of heat and cold. He recalls being in a white hotel lavatory with his father, where the faucets were marked hot and cold; he drinks hot tea as he wonders whether "all white things were cold and damp." When Wells, the boy who pushed him, teases him about kissing his mother, Stephen feels "hot and confused." In the chapel, which has a "cold night smell," the boy imagines sleeping before the fireplace of one of the cottages in the nearby village of Clane. In reverse of the bedwetting in the novel's opening paragraphs, Stephen thinks about the pleasant sensation of the bedsheets getting "warmer and warmer till he felt warm all over, ever so warm." Still, he cannot help thinking about the darkness surrounding him: "All the dark was cold and strange," he thinks, and then falls asleep dreaming of the warmth and cheer of the holidays.

The next morning, Stephen is taken to the school infirmary to recover from his illness. There he meets a friendly boy named Athy, whose father owns racehorses and who, in contrast to Stephen, takes delight in his own "queer name." He also meets Brother Michael, a kindly cleric in charge of the infirmary, who provides company for the sick boys by reading the daily newspaper aloud. Stephen comforts himself by imagining the "beautiful and sad" burial ceremony the school would hold for him and Wells's remorse over having caused his death. He falls into a fitful sleep in which thoughts of his own death flow into Brother Michael's reading of the newspaper account of Parnell's death. This section closes with Stephen's dream of Dante at Parnell's funeral, "in a maroon velvet dress and with a green velvet mantle . . . walking proudly and silently past the people who knelt by the water's edge."

The third section of **chapter one** opens with another image of red and green, a "great fire, banked high and red" and a chandelier decked in ivy. Stephen is home for the Christmas holiday, and for the first time he is permitted to sit at the dinner table with the adults and not in the nursery with his younger brothers and sisters.

The Christmas dinner scene in *A Portrait of the Artist* is widely acknowledged as one of the strongest in the novel. The event marks a pivotal moment in young Stephen's life. At the same time that he is initiated into the world of adults, he learns that this world is not what it seems. In the fierce, vindictive political and religious argument between Simon Dedalus's friend John Casey and Dante, Stephen begins to realize that adulthood is not all excitement and joy, as he once believed; it is instead filled with anger, pain, and sorrow. Nor are adults themselves always what they appear to be. His beloved Dante is hostile and rigid; the normally jovial Mr. Casey is scornful and vulgar; even Stephen's father, Simon, behaves differently. This experience is the first of many in which Stephen gradually becomes disillusioned with what he once believed was sacred—family, country, and religion.

In the next scene Stephen, having returned to Clongowes, listens while his schoolmates discuss the fate of a group of boys accused of stealing wine from the sacristy of the church. Athy believes that they have also been caught engaging in homosexual behavior. The boys watch a cricket game as they talk; the players look "smaller and farther away" because Stephen is not wearing his glasses. They were broken the previous day when a sprinter knocked him over. As he listens to the sound of the cricketbat and the discussion of how the errant boys will be punished, he wonders what the pain of a pandybat or cane would feel like.

Back inside during Father Arnall's Latin lesson, Father Dolan, the prefect of studies, enters the classroom. Relentless in his desire to punish "lazy idle little schemers," Father Dolan pandies Stephen for not writing his Latin assignment, even though the boy was exempted from work while he waited for a new pair of eyeglasses to arrive. Again, Stephen learns that all authority figures are not necessarily judicious, and for the first time he experiences the surprising cruelty and unfairness of the Catholic Church, as represented by Father Dolan:

> He felt the touch of the prefect's fingers as they had steadied his hand and at first he had thought that he was going to shake hands with him because the fingers were soft and firm: but then in an instant, he had heard the swish of the soutane sleeve and the crash.

An unexpected outcome of Stephen's punishment is that he begins to feel camaraderie with his classmates. During meal-time in the refectory, they encourage him to appeal to the rector before he is wrongly punished again by Dolan. At their urging, Stephen summons the courage to follow—much like his namesake, Daedalus—the labyrinthine hallways of the "castle," where Father Conmee's office is located. His meeting ulti-mately proves successful: the rector promises to speak to Father Dolan about the incident. For the moment, Stephen has conquered his attackers and has become a hero to his peers. The whole world now seems softer and more agreeable.

Stephen's distrust for authority figures grows in **chapter two**. He has returned home for the summer; his family has moved from Bray to Blackrock, near Dublin. As the chapter opens, he is spending time with his great-uncle Charles, who smokes a foul-smelling tobacco known as "black twist." Stephen enjoys taking daily walks through town with Uncle Charles, after which they stop at the park, where Simon Dedalus's friend Mike Flynn trains Stephen to be a runner. Although Mr. Dedalus claims that Flynn "had put some of the best runners of modern times through his hands," Stephen doubts his father's words as he looks at the man's "flabby stubblecovered face" and his "long stained fingers" that roll his cigarettes. On the way home, Stephen and Uncle Charles visit a nearby chapel, where the old man piously prays; but the boy does not share his uncle's piety and does not quite understand why the old man prays "so seriously."

Every Sunday, Stephen accompanies his father and Uncle Charles on their "constitutional" and listens carefully to their family stories and discussions about Irish politics. Although he does not always understand what they are saying, Stephen feels closer to the adult world as he listens to them. In the evenings, he enjoys reading Alexandre Dumas's *The Count of Monte Cristo* and delights in its romantic language, fancying himself a character from the novel.

At the end of the summer, Stephen is relieved to learn that he will not return to Clongowes; however, he also discovers with trepidation that the reason has to do with his father's mounting debts: "In a vague way he understood that his father was in trouble. . . . For some time he had felt the slight changes in his house; and these changes in what he had deemed unchangeable were so many slight shocks to his boyish conception of the world."

Shortly after, the family moves once more from the relative comfort of Blackrock to a "bare cheerless house" in the city of Dublin. Here, through a conversation at the dinner table, Stephen learns that his school victory over Father Dolan was illusory. Mr. Dedalus reduces Stephen's heroic encounter with Father Conmee to a joke told over dinner. The rector and Father Dolan, Mr. Dedalus says, "had a great laugh over it." Conmee teases his fellow priest by warning him, "*You better mind yourself, Father Dolan . . . or young Dedalus will send you up for twice nine.* We had a famous laugh together over it. Ha! Ha! Ha!"

The next scene takes place more than two years later, when Stephen is an adolescent, about fourteen years old. He is finishing his second year at Belvedere, where he has become an outstanding student, essay writer, and actor. Stephen holds a "chief part" in the second half of a theater program presented by Belvedere students. While waiting for his cue outside the theater, he converses with two other second-year students, Wallis and Heron (here Joyce introduces another bird image, as Stephen thinks it is "strange that Vincent Heron had a bird's face as well as a bird's name"). The classmates tease him by mentioning that they saw Mr. Dedalus entering the theater and being questioned about his son's performance by a girl whom Stephen admires. Stephen grows annoyed at the joking: "For him there was nothing amusing in a girl's interest and regard."

Stephen's sense of his own exile increases in other ways as well. He admires a girl named Emma Cleary but is unable to express himself to her. He begins to revel in his solitude: "The noise of the children at play annoyed him and their silly voices made him feel, even more keenly than he had felt at Clongowes, that he was different from the others." Stephen balks at his schoolmates' crude banter about his interest in Emma, even as he is defiant in his insistence to them that Byron is a poet superior to Tennyson. The boys taunt Stephen with the word "admit" that recalls the baby Stephen's instructions to "apologise" in the first section.

While growing ever estranged from his family and the rest of the world, Stephen accompanies Simon Dedalus on a trip to Cork, the senior Dedalus's birthplace, where the increasingly impoverished Simon plans to sell a plot of land. Stephen listens "without sympathy to his father's evocation of Cork and of the scenes of his youth. . . . Stephen heard but could feel no pity." Stephen and his father wander into the anatomy theater of the Queen's College building, where Mr. Dedalus had been a medical student. While Mr. Dedalus searches for his initials on a desk, Stephen recoils in horror upon finding the word *Foetus* carved on a desk:

> The letters cut in the stained wood of the desk stared upon him, mocking his bodily weakness and futile enthusiasms and making him loathe himself for his own mad and filthy orgies. The spittle in his throat grew bitter and foul to swallow and the faint sickness climbed to his brain so that for a moment he closed his eyes and walked on in darkness.

Riddled with guilt over his own masturbation, which is surely incomprehensible to him, Stephen is then jolted by a lecture about the body, which boldly contrasts the institutional speech of the school:

Stephen is convinced that his mortal sin is unique, utterly separate from his father's idealized memories of his own adolescence. He tunes out his father by reciting to himself three lines from Shelley's poetic fragment "To the Moon." Poetry serves as a comfort to the confused Stephen, who will later look toward art as a key to liberation from such guilt.

After Stephen returns from Cork, his lust proves to be as overpowering as a raging river: "their forms began once more to jostle fiercely above the crumbled mole." He longs to escape from the world of coldness he associates with the fathers, and longs for the darkness and warmth he associates with the mother's womb from which he emerges in the novel's first paragraph. The "orgies" he described earlier in the chapter were merely masturbatory; the chapter ends with Stephen wanting "to sin with another of his kind, to force another being to sin with him and to exult with her in sin." The sixteen-year-old Stephen wanders to the Jewish quarter where he goes to a whorehouse to lose his virginity. The "tears of joy" he sheds when he embraces the whore indicate that he has yet to reach full maturity. Yet his sense of guilt about sex is realized nevertheless:

> He closed his eyes, surrendering himself to her, body and mind, conscious of nothing in the world but the dark pressure of her softly parting lips. They pressed upon his brain as upon his lips as though they were the vehicle of a vague speech; and between them he felt an unknown and timid pressure, darker than the swoon of sin, softer than sound or odour.

The "vague speech" is, of course, the speech of the body represented in the opening paragraph of the novel. For a moment, the attack on Stephen recedes, and the initial warmth that baby Stephen experienced occurs again: Stephen's descent into darkness suggests his reentering the womb.

The opening of **chapter three** indicates a sharp retreat from Stephen's blissful epiphany. Stephen's lesson in the opening scene is repeated, as the pleasure of the "warm calm rise and fall of [the whore's] breast" is followed immediately by this passage:

> The swift December dusk had come tumbling clownishly after its dull day and as he stared through the dull square of the window of the schoolroom he felt his belly crave for its food. He hoped there would be stew for dinner, turnips and carrots and bruised potatoes and fat mutton pieces to be ladled out in thick peppered flourfattened sauce. Stuff it into you, his belly counseled him.

It would be hard to imagine that Joyce, who would prove himself to be among the greatest master of puns in his later work, was unaware of the contrast of warmth and cold between the closing image of sexual warmth in chapter two and the opening image of the "swift December dusk" that begins chapter three. Indeed, what had seemed liberating in the previous chapter has been transformed into the world of the grossly physical. The lust that drives him to be "awakened from a slumber of centuries" has become the mere business of appetite, and Stephen's raging passions are "quenched: and the cold darkness filled chaos."

Stephen then goes to a religious retreat where he is frightened into chastity by the relentless sermon of Father Arnall, who had been one of Stephen's teachers at Clongowes. In descriptions that recall Dante's *Inferno* in their detailed descriptions of Hell, Stephen reacts to Father Arnall's attack the same way he has reacted to every other experience: he believes it is directed specifically at him.

> Every sense of the flesh is tortured and every faculty of the soul therewith: the eyes with impenetrable utter darkness, the nose with noisome odours, the ears with yells and howls and execrations, the taste with foul matter, leprous corruption, nameless suffocating filth, the touch with redhot goads and spikes, with cruel tongues of flame. And through the several torments of the senses and the immortal soul is tortured eternally in its very

essence amid the leagues upon leagues of glowing fires kindled in the abyss by the offended majesty of the Omnipotent God and fanned into everlasting and ever increasing fury by the breath of anger of the Godhead.

For a writer whose artistic vision is Aristotelian—dependent on the senses above all else—such a mortification of senses would indeed pose the most frightening torture imaginable. Stephen is terrified when he learns that, according to the priest, in order to save himself he must suppress the natural aspects of experience that he has thus far embraced. Upon returning to Dublin, Stephen is consumed with self-hatred, fearing that his trysts have reduced his soul to "black cold void waste." He experiences the kind of Aristotelian pity and terror about which he will write an aesthetic theory in chapter five. Finally, after a confession with a bearded priest who admonishes him to avoid a sin that "kills the body and . . . soul," Stephen is absolved and receives communion, overwhelmed by the prospects of living "a live of grace and virtue and happiness!"

Of course, such a regimen is anticlimactic once instituted. **Chapter four** begins with a deflation of the triumphant tone that closed chapter three. The idea of a sinless life is stultifying, and his life is reduced to self-imposed ritual and habit which "did not wholly reward his zeal of prayer since he could never know how much temporal punishment he had remitted by way of suffrage for the agonising souls." Stephen's newfound piety is tantamount to a "surrender" to all the attackers—from the schoolboys' taunts to the priest's pandying—who attempted to destroy his developing soul. Stephen's Jesuit demeanor is so convincing that the director of Belvedere College thinks Stephen is one of the few boys fit for the priesthood. He tells him, "Perhaps you are the boy in this college whom God designs to call Himself." Stephen imagines himself as "The Reverend Stephen Dedalus, S.J.," but is immediately discomforted with the idea and rejects it. He becomes painfully aware of the "frail hold which so many years of order and obedience had of him when once a definite and irrevocable act of his threatened to end for ever, in time and in eternity, his freedom."

Stephen begins to realize that his fall from such forced grace is inevitable. The Dedalus family, meanwhile, is undergoing its own fall from grace in the form of a downward economic spiral, which becomes apparent when Stephen asks his sister indignantly, "Why are we on the move again, if it's a fair question?" Stephen is able to escape from his family's woes to University College, Dublin. The intellectual freedom of the university allows him to ponder his own ambivalence about his purported calling to the priesthood, and to question all forms of authority: "The end he had been born to serve yet did not see had led him to escape by an unseen path: and now it beckoned to him once more and a new adventure was about to be opened to him."

As Stephen kills his devotion to the Christian God, it becomes unclear to him what it is he will worship. Walking along the shore, Stephen hears ironic plays on his name ("Stephanerous Dedalos! Bous Stephanoumenos!") that remind him of his exile from his Irish peers. But the mythical implications of his name are suddenly revealed to him in the beginning of what becomes the central epiphany of the novel: "Now, as never before, his strange name seemed to him a prophecy." It is revealed to Stephen in a flash that he had been meant to be a priest of art rather than a priest of God, "a symbol of the artist forging anew in his workshop out of the sluggish manner of the earth a new soaring impalpable being."

A vision of a girl brings this epiphany even higher. Inasmuch as the idea of "mixed bathing" was taboo in turn-of-the-century Ireland, her bare legs indicate a rebellion against the repressive Catholicism from which Stephen must revolt. In an image that synthesizes the erotic with the secularly spiritual, Stephen is brought to his greatest point of blissful self-realization:

> Her image had passed into his soul for ever and no word had broken the holy silence of his ecstasy. Her eyes had called him and his soul had leaped at the call. To live, to err, to fall, to triumph, to recreate life out of life!

His metaphoric rebirth recalls the initial wonder and fear of the infant in the first paragraph of the novel. Stephen is discovering the world anew, freed from his attackers, and ready to become an artist.

The epiphany of chapter four, like all other epiphanies in the novel, is followed by disappointment. **Chapter five** begins with Stephen's moment of aesthetic glory defeated, a long way from his previous triumph. As in the opening of chapter three, Stephen stoically endures a poor man's meal: watery tea and fried bread, with a box of pawn tickets strewn on the table. Stephen is a cynical college student eager to prove his intellectual maturity, but the image of his mother washing his ears belies such a stance. After Stephen scoffs at his father's reference to his brother as a "bitch," Mrs. Dedalus recognizes and points out the change in her son: "'Ah, it's a scandalous shame for you, Stephen,' said his mother, 'and you'll live to rue the day you set foot in that place. I know how it has changed you.'" Stephen is finally standing up to his attackers, but his sense of exile increases, suggesting that his struggle for autonomy is far from over.

Stephen attempts to write a poem, but it is a failure. Later, in a philosophy class, Stephen previews his attempts to outdo the *Poetics* of Aristotle, an ancient Greek philosopher whose manual about tragedy is widely regarded as the birth of literary criticism. After the class breaks up into sophomoric chaos, the boys continue their discussion alone. Each one of Stephen's friends identifies with a particular issue: Cranly with Darwinism, Davin with Irish patriotism, and McAnn with feminism (which Moynihan reduces to "No stimulants and votes for the bitches"). Stephen, meanwhile, is taken with the loftier questions of the noble and the beautiful. Like the boys at Belvedere who beat him for preferring Byron to Tennyson, his University College classmates weary of Stephen's stubborn individualism. When Davin tells Stephen to "be one of us" and learn the Irish language, Stephen dismisses the idea. Later, he makes a bitter reference to the "moocow" of the book's opening by denigrating Ireland as "the old sow that eats her farrow." Finally, with characteristic audacity, Stephen claims "Aristotle has not defined pity and terror. I have." What follows is not an improvement upon the thinking of the founder of aesthetics, but an undergraduate's posturings, suggesting that Stephen has escaped from the orthodoxy of the church only to be held hostage by the orthodoxy of the intellect.

The next morning, Stephen awakens from a nocturnal emission: "Towards dawn he awoke. O what sweet music! His soul was all dewy wet." Emma Cleary reappears, and they have a brief, enigmatic exchange. Stephen finally finishes his villanelle, showing promise, but still lacking the artistic spark for which he is waiting. In a conversation with Cranly, Stephen comes closer than ever before to revealing himself. What begins as a polite interview turns into a psychoanalytic catechism, and Stephen is brutally honest. At one point, Cranly asks Stephen "Do you love your mother?" recalling the Clongowes boys' taunts of "Do you kiss your mother?" When asked how many siblings he had, Stephen gives this astonishing reply: "Nine or ten. . . . Some died." Finally, Stephen pledges his *non serviam*, recalling Satan's rebellion from God:

> I will not serve that in which I no longer believe whether it call itself my home, my fatherland, or my church: and I will try to express myself in some mode of life or art as freely as I can and as wholly as I can, using for my defence the only arms I allow myself to use, silence, exile and cunning.

At twenty, Stephen's new incarnation will be the bohemian expatriate, who must leave the restrictions of home to find his artistic voice. Freed from the attacks of father figures, Stephen must become his own father.

The final section of the novel is written in the form of diary entries, suggesting a return to the fragmented form of the beginning of the book. Most of what is described is uneventful: talks about politics, writing, and walking along Dublin's streets. The cyclical turns the novel has taken appear to be endless, and the novel's circular retreat to fragmentation suggests an aesthetic of dissonance. Still, Stephen is given an astonishing entry toward the end of the work, suggesting that greatness awaits him in the future:

26 April: Mother is putting my new secondhand clothes in order. She prays now, she says, that I may learn what the heart is and what it feels. Amen. So be it. Welcome, O life! I go to encounter for the millionth time the reality of experience and to forge in the smithy of my soul the uncreated conscience of my race.

27 April: Old father, old artificer, stand me now and ever in good stead.

At the beginning of the novel, Stephen identifies his mother with a song and his father with a story. At the end, he turns again to his mother to understand abstract emotion, while looking toward his father for coherence. Joyce's novel evokes more of the abstract emotion of the mother's song than the logic of the father's story, although the novel does have a logic of its own. Stephen must leave Ireland to acquire humanity and wisdom, and his story is continued in *Ulysses*, a far more complete, complex work that established Joyce as the strongest of modern novelists. At the close of *A Portrait of the Artist*, we leave Stephen between adolescence and adulthood. ❖

List of Characters

Stephen Dedalus is the introverted, bitter, ironic, and often narcissistic protagonist who must conquer the attacks from Roman Catholicism in order to become the "artist" of the book's title. Young Stephen, who is left on his own to cope with the stern discipline of Jesuit schools, feels isolated from his family. He begins his adolescence with visits to whorehouses but is frightened into chastity by a terrifying sermon by Father Arnall. After enduring a self-imposed monklike regimen as penance for his sins, he is tapped for the priesthood by the Jesuit officer. But feeling discomfort with the thought of being "The Reverend Stephen Dedalus, S.J.," Stephen runs to a beach, sees a vision of a beautiful girl, and realizes he must be an artist. Following a doctrine of secular aestheticism, Stephen becomes a sarcastic, priggish scholar who impresses his friends and teachers with his intellect but remains in solitude, clinging to his weapons of "silence, exile, and cunning."

Simon Dedalus is the father of Stephen. Mr. Dedalus is usually benevolent to Stephen, but Stephen is only able to see his father as a threat to his autonomy. Mr. Dedalus is unable to understand his son's inner life, and the gap between them is apparent. Modeled after the experiences of Joyce's own father, Mr. Dedalus's declining financial fortunes have an impact on Stephen; the ironic Stephen of chapter five describes Mr. Dedalus as "a bankrupt and at present a praiser of his own past."

Father Arnall is Stephen's teacher at Clongowes Wood College. He exempts Stephen from his studies when his glasses are accidentally broken, then later frightens the adolescent Stephen with a terrifying sermon about Hell. It is Father Arnall's sermon that inspires Stephen's brief religious conversion.

Father Dolan is the prefect of studies at Clongowes Wood College, who unjustly "pandies" Stephen for accidentally breaking his glasses, and puts the fear of God into every "lazy little schemer." At the urging of his friends, Stephen appeals to

Father Comnee, who finally speaks with Father Dolan about the incident.

Uncle Charles is the doddering, comforting presence who was a constant companion to young Stephen and inspired Hugh Kenner's discovery of the "Uncle Charles Principle," in which Joyce uses his narrative to depict the language of others. (In one scene, Joyce uses the word "repaired" the way Uncle Charles, not the author, would use it.)

Cranly is Stephen's friend from University College, Dublin, who conducts an interview with him that produces Stephen's most intimate dialogue.

Emma Cleary is the girl for whose affections Stephen longs throughout much of the novel. Emma inspires a poem that Stephen finally finishes toward the end of the book. ❖

Critical Views

EDWARD GARNETT ON *A PORTRAIT* IN NEED OF POLISH

[Edward Garnett (1868–1936), a poet, playwright, novelist, and critic, is chiefly remembered as a reviewer and patron of some of the great writers of the early twentieth century, including Joseph Conrad and D. H. Lawrence. Among his critical works are *Tolstoy: His Life and Writings* (1914). In this reader's report for Duckworth & Co., Publishers, Garnett calls *A Portrait of the Artist* well written but in need of revision.]

James Joyce's "Portrait of the Artist as a Young Man" wants going through carefully from start to finish. There are many "longueurs." Passages which, though the publisher's reader may find them entertaining, will be tedious to the ordinary man among the reading public. That public will call the book, as it stands at present, realistic, unprepossessing, unattractive. We call it ably written. The picture is "curious," it arouses interest and attention. But the author must revise it and let us see it again. It is too discursive, formless, unrestrained, and ugly things, ugly words, are too prominent; indeed at times they seem to be shoved in one's face, on purpose, unnecessarily. The point of view will be voted "a little sordid." The picture of life is good; the period well brought to the reader's eye, and the types and characters are well drawn, but it is too "unconventional." This would stand against it in normal times. At the present time, though the old conventions are in the background, we can only see a chance for it if it is pulled into shape and made more definite.

In the earlier portion of the MS. as submitted to us, a good deal of pruning can be done. Unless the author will use restraint and proportion he will not gain readers. His pen and his thoughts seem to have run away with him sometimes.

And at the end of the book there is a complete falling to bits; the pieces of writing and the thoughts are all in pieces and they fall like damp, ineffective rockets.

The author shows us he had art, strength and originality, but this MS. wants time and trouble spent on it, to make it a more finished piece of work, to shape it more carefully as the product of craftsmanship, mind and imagination of an artist.

—Edward Garnett, "Reader's Report of *A Portrait of the Artist as a Young Man*," (1916, reprint in *Letters of James Joyce*, ed. Richard Ellmann, London: Faber and Faber, 1966), pp. 371–72

H. G. WELLS ON THE MERITS AND POLITICS OF *A PORTRAIT OF THE ARTIST*

[H. G. Wells (1866–1944), the vastly prolific English novelist and essayist, was also an ardent critic and reviewer. In the following extract, Wells praises Joyce's experimental style and believable protagonist, as well as his realistic and detailed description of an Irish-Catholic upbringing.]

[*A Portrait of the Artist as a Young Man*] is a book to buy and read and lock up, but it is not a book to miss. Its claim to be literature is as good as the claim of the last book of *Gulliver's Travels*.

It is no good trying to minimize a characteristic that seems to be deliberately obtruded. Like Swift and another living Irish writer, Mr. Joyce has a cloacal obsession. He would bring back into the general picture of life aspects which modern drainage and modern decorum have taken out of ordinary intercourse and conversation. Coarse, unfamiliar words are scattered about the book unpleasantly, and it may seem to many, needlessly. If the reader is squeamish upon these matters, then there is nothing for it but to shun this book, but if he will pick his way, as one has to do at times on the outskirts of some picturesque

Italian village with a view and a church and all sorts of things of that sort to tempt one, then it is quite worth while. And even upon this unsavory aspect of Swift and himself, Mr. Joyce is suddenly illuminating. He tells at several points how his hero Stephen is swayed and shocked and disgusted by harsh and loud *sounds*, and how he is stirred to intense emotion by music and the rhythms of beautiful words. But no sort of smell offends him like that. He finds olfactory sensations interesting or aesthetically displeasing, but they do not make him sick or excited as sounds do. This is a quite understandable turn over from the more normal state of affairs. Long ago I remember pointing out in a review the difference in the sensory basis of the stories of Robert Louis Stevenson and Sir J. M. Barrie; the former visualized and saw his story primarily as a picture, the latter mainly heard it. We shall do Mr. Joyce an injustice if we attribute a normal sensory basis to him and then accuse him of deliberate offense.

But this is by the way. The value of Mr. Joyce's book has little to do with its incidental insanitary condition. Like some of the best novels in the world it is the story of an education; it is by far the most living and convincing picture that exists of an Irish Catholic upbringing. It is a mosaic of jagged fragments that does altogether render with extreme completeness the growth of a rather secretive, imaginative boy in Dublin. The technique is startling, but on the whole it succeeds. Like so many Irish writers from Sterne to Shaw Mr. Joyce is a bold experimentalist with paragraph and punctuation. He breaks away from scene to scene without a hint of the change of time and place; at the end he passes suddenly from the third person to the first; he uses no inverted commas to mark off his speeches < . . . > One conversation in this book is a superb success, the one in which Mr. Dedalus carves the Christmas turkey; I write with all due deliberation that Sterne himself could not have done it better; but most of the talk flickers blindingly with these dashes, one has the same wincing feeling of being flicked at that one used to have in the early cinema shows. I think Mr. Joyce has failed to discredit the inverted comma.

The interest of the book depends entirely upon its quintessential and unfailing reality. One believes in Stephen Dedalus as one believes in few characters in fiction. And the peculiar lie of the interest for the intelligent reader is the convincing revelation it makes of the limitations of a great mass of Irishmen. Mr. Joyce tells us unsparingly of the adolescence of this youngster under conditions that have passed almost altogether out of English life. There is an immense shyness, a profound secrecy, about matters of sex, with its inevitable accompaniment of nightmare revelations and furtive scribblings in unpleasant places, and there is a living belief in a real hell. The description of Stephen listening without a doubt to two fiery sermons on that tremendous theme, his agonies of fear, not disgust at dirtiness such as unorthodox children feel but just fear, his terror-inspired confession of his sins of impurity to a strange priest in a distant part of the city, is like nothing in any boy's experience who has been trained under modern conditions. Compare its stuffy horror with Conrad's account of how under analogous circumstances Lord Jim wept. And a second thing of immense significance is the fact that everyone in this Dublin story, every human being, accepts as a matter of course, as a thing in nature like the sky and the sea, that the English are to be hated. There is no discrimination in that hatred, there is no gleam of recognition that a considerable number of Englishmen have displayed a very earnest disposition to put matters right with Ireland, there is an absolute absence of any idea of a discussed settlement, any notion of helping the slow-witted Englishman in his three-cornered puzzle between North and South. It is just hate, a cant cultivated to the pitch of monomania, an ungenerous violent direction of the mind. That is the political atmosphere in which Stephen Dedalus grows up, and in which his essentially responsive mind orients itself. I am afraid it is only too true an account of the atmosphere in which a number of brilliant young Irishmen have grown up. What is the good of pretending that the extreme Irish "patriot" is an equivalent and parallel of the English or American liberal? He is narrower and intenser than any English Tory. He will be the natural ally of the Tory in delaying British social and economic reconstruction after the war. He will play into the hands of the Tories by threatening an outbreak and providing the excuse for a militarist reaction in England. It is time the American observer faced the truth of that. No reason in that why England should not do justice to Ireland, but excellent reason for bearing in mind that these bright-green young people across the Channel are something quite different from the liberal English in training and tradition, and absolutely set against helping them. No single book has ever shown how different they are, as completely as this most memorable novel.

—H. G. Wells, "James Joyce," (1917; reprint in *James Joyce: The Critical Heritage*, ed. Robert H. Deming, London: Routledge & Kegan Paul, 1970), pp. 86–88

EZRA POUND ON JOYCE'S FLAUBERTIAN PROSE

[Ezra Pound (1885–1972) was an extremely influential modernist poet and a founder, with Hilda Doolittle and others, of the Imagist movement in poetry. An influential critic, Pound was also a tireless champion of other modern writers, including T. S. Eliot and James Joyce. His critical essays were collected in 1954 in *Literary Essays of Ezra Pound*. In the following extract, Pound compares Joyce's realistic style to that of the French novelist Gustave Flaubert.]

The last few years have seen the gradual shaping of a party of intelligence, a party not bound by any central doctrine or theory. We cannot accurately define new writers by applying to them tag-names from old authors, but as there is no adequate means of conveying the general impression of their characteristics one may at times employ such terminology, carefullly stating that the terms are nothing more than approximation.

With that qualification, I would say that James Joyce produces the nearest thing to Flaubertian prose that we have now in English, just as Wyndham Lewis has written a novel which is more like, and more fitly compared with, Dostoievsky than is the work of any of his contemporaries. In like manner Mr. T. S. Eliot comes nearer to filling the place of Jules La

Forgue in our generation. (Doing the "nearest thing" need not imply an approach to a standard, from a position inferior.)

⟨. . . .⟩ I am, perhaps, fairly safe in reasserting Joyce's ability as a writer. It will cost me no more than a few violent attacks from sheltered, and therefore courageous, anonymities. When you tell the Irish that they are slow in recognizing their own men of genius they reply with street riots and politics.

Now, despite the jobbing of bigots and their sectarian publishing houses, and despite the "Fly-Fishers" and the types which they represent, and despite the unwillingness of the print-packers (a word derived from pork-packers) and the initial objections of the Dublin publishers and the later unwillingness of the English publishers, Mr. Joyce's novel appears in book form, and intelligent readers gathering few by few will read it, and it will remain a permanent part of English literature— written by an Irishman in Trieste and first published in New York City. I doubt if a comparison of Mr. Joyce to other English writers or Irish writers would help much to define him. One can only say that he is rather unlike them. *The Portrait* is very different from *L'Education Sentimentale*, but it would be easier to compare it with that novel of Flaubert's than with anything else. Flaubert pointed out that if France had studied his work they might have been saved a good deal in 1870. If more people had read *The Portrait* and certain stories in Mr. Joyce's *Dubliners* there might have been less recent trouble in Ireland. A clear diagnosis is never without its value.

Apart from Mr. Joyce's realism—the school-life, the life in the University, the family dinner with the discussion of Parnell depicted in his novel—apart from, or of a piece with, all this is the style, the actual writing: hard, clear-cut, with no waste of words, no bundling up of useless phrases, no filling in with pages of slosh.

—Ezra Pound, "At Last the Novel Apppears," (1917; reprint in *Pound/Joyce*, ed. Forrest Read, New York: New Directions, 1965), pp. 89–90

AN ANONYMOUS REVIEWER ON *PORTRAIT OF THE ARTIST AS A YOUNG MAN*

[In an early review from the *Irish Book Lover*, a critic praises Joyce's engaging style and plot and his adept handling of dialogue, but objects to his use of offensive language and excessive realism.]

In spite of the serious drawbacks to be mentioned later, truth compels one to admit that this pseudo autobiography of Stephen Dedalus, a weakling and a dreamer, makes fascinating reading. We read it at a single sitting. The hero's schooldays at Clongowes Wood, and later at Belvedere, are graphically and doubtless, faithfully portrayed, as is the visit to Cork in company with his father, a clever ne'er-do-well, gradually sinking in the social scale. One of the strongest scenes in the book is the description of the Christmas dinner party during the black year of 1891, when Nationalist Ireland was riven to the centre over the Parnell "split." Mr. Joyce is unsparing in his realism, and his violent contrasts—the brothel, the confessional—jar on one's finer feelings. So do the quips and jeers of the students, in language unprinted in literature since the days of Swift and Sterne, following on some eloquent and orthodox sermons! That Mr. Joyce is a master of a brilliant descriptive style and handles his dialogue as ably as any living writer is conceded on all hands, and oh! the pity of it. In writing thus he is just to his fine gifts? Is it even wise, from a worldly point of view—mercenary, if you will—to dissipate one's talents on a book which can only attain a limited circulation?—for no clean-minded person could possibly allow it to remain within reach of his wife, his sons or daughters. Above all, is it Art? We doubt it.

—Unsigned, review of *A Portrait of the Artist as a Young Man* by James Joyce, *Irish Booklover* 8, No. 9–8 (April–May 1917): 113

John C. Squire on Joyce as a True Realist

[John C. Squire (1884–1958), a poet, parodist, editor, and critic, founded the *London Mercury* in 1919 and gained considerable influence as literary editor of the *New Statesman* and chief literary critic of the *Observer*. Some of his essays were published under the pseudonym Solomon Eagle. In the following extract, taken from a collection of essays entitled *Books in General by Solomon Eagle* (1919), Squire praises Joyce as a "realist of the first order," who remains completely detached from his autobiographical hero.]

You recognize its individuality in the very first paragraph [of *A Portrait of the Artist as a Young Man*]. Mr. Joyce tries to put down the vivid and incoherent memories of childhood in a vivid and incoherent way: to show one Stephen Dedalus's memories precisely as one's own memories might appear if one ransacked one's mind ⟨. . . .⟩ There is verisimilitude in this; but a critic on the look-out for Mr. Joyce's idiosyncrasies would certainly fasten upon his preoccupation with the olfactory— which sometimes leads him to write things he might as well have left to be guessed at—as one of them. Still, it is a minor characteristic. His major characteristics are his intellectual integrity, his sharp eyes, and his ability to set down precisely what he wants to set down. He is a realist of the first order. You feel that he means to allow no personal prejudice or predilection to distort the record of what he sees. His perceptions may be naturally limited; but his honesty in registering their results is complete. It is even a little too complete. There are some things that we are all familiar with and that ordinary civilized manners (not pharisaism) prevent us from importing into general conversation ⟨. . . .⟩

He is a genuine realist: that is to say, he puts in the exaltations as well as the depressions, the inner life as well as the outer. He is not morosely determined to paint everything drab. Spiritual passions are as powerful to him as physical passions; and as far as his own bias goes it may as well be in favor of Catholic asceticism as of sensual materialism. For his detachment as author is almost inhuman. If Stephen is himself, then he is a self who is expelled and impartially scrutinized, without pity or "allowances," directly [as] Mr. Joyce the artist gets to work. And of the other characters one may say that they are always given their due, always drawn so as to evoke the sympathy they deserve, yet are never openly granted the sympathy of the author. He is the outsider, the observer, the faithful selector of significant traits, moral and physical; his judgments, if he forms them, are concealed. He never even shows by a quiver of the pen that anything distresses him ⟨. . . .⟩

This is not everybody's book. The later portion, consisting largely of rather dull student discussions, is dull; nobody could be inspired by the story, and it had better be neglected by any one who is easily disgusted. Its interest is mainly technical, using the word in its broadest sense; and its greatest appeal, consequently, is made to the practising artist in literature. What Mr. Joyce will do with his powers in the future it is impossible to conjecture. I conceive that he does not know himself: that, indeed the discovery of a form is the greatest problem in front of him. It is doubtful if he will make a novelist.

—John C. Squire, "Mr. James Joyce," *Books in General by Solomon Eagle* (New York: Alfred A. Knopf, 1919), pp. 246, 247–48, 249–50

HERBERT S. GORMAN ON *A PORTRAIT OF THE ARTIST* AS OBJECTIVE AUTOBIOGRAPHY

[Herbert S. Gorman (1893-1954) was a novelist and an influential literary critic. Among his publications are *Hawthorne: A Study in Solitude* (1927) and *A Victorian American: Henry Wadsworth Longfellow* (1926). In the following extract, taken from *James Joyce: His first Forty Years* (1926), Gorman explores the autobiographical nature of *A Portrait of the Artist* and the power with which Joyce reveals Stephen Dadalus's inner life.]

"A Portrait of the Artist as a Young Man," of course, is autobiography. Indeed, the progress of Joyce's mind since *Dubliners* has been almost wholly autobiographical. Most of the time he is concerned with himself and his reactions to environment. The emphasis is on spiritual environment. With this for his subject-matter Joyce set out with his new technique and delivered himself of a novel that is mainly subjective but which is starred with the most distinguished objective pictures. The story is one of the boyhood and youth of Stephen Dedalus, an Irishman brought up and educated by Jesuits. Stephen is sensitive, brooding, and delicately cerebrated. Upon the clear slate of his consciousness his environment draws dark and forbidding lines. His boyhood is unusual insomuch as it is an unending stream of personal reactions to even the lightest touches of the existence into which he has been flung. The unique qualities of the novel are to be found in the revelation of the youth's unspoken thoughts, the setting down of the sometimes unconscious stream with a cold candor and deliberate frankness that was not to be found in the fiction of its day. There is a Rousseau-like self-flagellation in some of this material. We cannot doubt that. Joyce is turning himself inside out, spilling forth all the jangled moods that lie deep in artistic consciousness. The sensibilities of Stephen Dedalus are evidenced in such magnificent chapters as the religious retreat where the horrors of Hell are pictured by a priest and before whom the boy grovels in the intense fanatic-grip of his faith, in the long talk with Lynch in which Stephen outlines his aesthetic theories, and in the last beautiful chapters where Stephen, now almost a man, passes through the white, torturing fire of his love-affair simultaneously with the realization that he has lost his faith.

In essence the book describes a formal, tawdry environment crushing a spirit that was born to be free, a spirit that will fight back and follow the flame which it sees dancing before it. Stephen knows that he is being crushed by a physical and intellectual leanness, that the props beneath him are rotten. As we witness the Dedalus family disintegrating throughout the pages of "A Portrait of the Artist as a Young Man" we observe, at the same time, the result of his gradual sinking in the muck on the sensitive mind of the young man. What progress can there be in a life like this for him? The gradual knowledge comes to him that he must leave it, that he must exile himself from it and long before those final pages when he eventually does prepare to leave Ireland it is quite perceptible that Stephen is an exile 〈. . . .〉 There are times when Joyce writes impartially but we feel that behind these impartial sentences there is a far from impartial man. In order to write so he must lift the scourge to his own back. Roman Catholicism is in his bones, in the beat of his blood, in the folds of his brain and he cannot rest until it is either removed or clarified. It is his misfortune that it may never be removed. It will pervert his nature (it does so in "Ulysses") but it is there, twisted out of all resemblance to itself even in the frankest passages. The vivid, highly-functioning mind of the Stephen Dedalus of "Portrait of the Artist as a Young Man" is the mind of a Mediæval Catholic. If the same mind had been twisted to the other side of the line it would have been to the intense visioning of a religiast.

—Herbert S. Gorman, *James Joyce: His First Forty Years* (London: Geoffrey Bles. 1926), pp. 72–74, 75

HARRY LEVIN ON JOYCE AS REALIST AND IMPRESSIONIST

[Harry Levin (1912–1994) was the Irving Babbitt Professor of Comparative Literature at Harvard University. Among his many publications are *The Broken Column: A Study in Romantic Hellenism* (1931) and *Symbolism and Function* (1956). In the following extract, taken from *James Joyce: A Critical Introduction* (1941), Levin explores Joyce's ability to build a linguistic bridge between realism and impressionism.]

Joyce's own contribution to English prose is to provide a more fluid medium for refracting sensations and impressions through the author's mind—to facilitate the transition from photographic realism to esthetic impressionism. In the introductory pages of the *Portrait of the Artist*, the reader is faced with nothing less than the primary impact of life itself, a presentational continuum of the tastes and smells and sights and sounds of earliest infancy. Emotion is integrated, from first to last, by words. Feelings, as they filter through Stephen's sensory apparatus, become associated with phrases. His conditioned reflexes are literary. In one of the later dialogues of the book, he is comparing his theory to a trimmed lamp. The dean of studies, taking up the metaphor, mentions the lamp of Epictetus, and Stephen's reply is a further allusion to the stoic doctrine that the soul is like a bucketful of water. In his mind this far-fetched chain of literary associations becomes attached to the sense impressions of the moment: "A smell of molten tallow came up from the dean's candle butts and fused itself into Stephen's consciousness with the jingle of words, bucket and lamp and lamp and bucket."

This is the state of mind that confers upon language a magical potency. It exalts the habit of verbal association into a principle for the arrangement of experience. You gain power over a thing by naming it; you become master of a situation by putting it into words. It is psychological need, and not hyperfastidious taste, that goads the writer on to search for the *mot juste*, to loot the thesaurus. Stephen, in the more explicit manuscript, finds a treasure-house in Skeat's *Etymological Dictionary*. The crucial moment of the book, which leads to the revelation of his name and calling, is a moment he tries to make his own by drawing forth a phrase of his treasure:

—A day of dappled seaborn clouds.—

The phrase and the day and the scene harmonised in a chord. Words. Was it their colours? He allowed them to glow and fade, hue after hue: sunrise gold, the russet and green of apple orchards, azure of waves, the greyfringed fleece of clouds. No, it was not their colours: it was the poise and balance of the period itself. Did he then love the rythmic rise and fall of words better than their associations of legend and colour? Or was it that, being as weak of sight as he was shy of mind, he drew less pleasure from the reflection of the glowing sensible world through the prism of a language manycoloured and richly storied than from the contemplation of an inner world of individual emotions mirrored perfectly in a lucid supple periodic prose.

The strength and weakness of his style, by Joyce's own diagnosis, are those of his mind and body. A few pages later he offers a cogent illustration, when Stephen dips self-consciously into his word-hoard for suitable epithets to describe a girl who is wading along the beach. We are given a paragraph of word-painting which is not easy to visualize. "Her bosom was as a bird's, soft and slight, slight and soft as the breast of some dark-plumaged dove," it concludes. "But her long fair hair was girlish: and girlish, and touched with the wonder of mortal beauty, her face." This is incantation, and not description. Joyce is thinking in rhythms rather than metaphors. Specification of the bird appeals to the sense of touch rather than to the sense of sight. What is said about the hair and the face is intended to produce an effect without presenting a picture. The most striking effects in Joyce's imagery are those of coldness, whiteness, and dampness, like the bodies of the bathers who shout Stephen's name.

—Harry Levin, *James Joyce: A Critical Introduction* (Norfolk, CT: New Directions, 1941), pp. 50–52

JAMES T. FARRELL ON THE BURDEN OF IRISH HISTORY IN JOYCE'S WORK

[James T. Farrell (1904–1979) was an American novelist and an important literary critic and reviewer. His works include *A Note on Literary Criticism* (1937) and *Literary Essays, 1954–1974* (1976). In the following extract, taken from *The League of Frightened Philistines and Other Papers* (1945), Farrell compares Stephen's attempts to escape "the paralysis of his Irish background to Joyce's own stylistic and literal exile from Ireland.]

What Stephen sees is Irish history in the present, in terms of what has happened to Ireland and to Irishmen as a result of their defeats. But Stephen does not dwell on a tragic past in moods of regret. Rather, he is bitter because of the condition of the Ireland he knows, the Ireland inherited from a tragic historic past. During the period when he was still at work on *A Portrait of the Artist as a Young Man*, Joyce, in a letter, describes Dublin as a "center of paralysis." It should be realized that it was Joyce who introduced the city realistically into modern Irish writing. The city—Dublin—is the focus of Ireland in his work, and in his life. We see that this is the case with Stephen, the genius son of a declassed family. Stephen lives, grows up in a Dublin that is a center of paralysis. Is he to have a future in such a center? Is he to prevent himself from suffering paralysis, spiritual paralysis? Stephen's painful burden of reality can be interpreted as a reality that derives from a history of Ireland's defeats and that is focused, concretized, in the very quality of the men of Dublin. Stephen describes his own father to a friend as "A medical student, an oarsman, a tenor, an amateur actor, a shouting politician, a small landlord, a small investor, a drinker, a good fellow, a storyteller, somebody's secretary, something in a distillery, a tax gatherer, a bankrupt, and at present a praiser of his own past." Just as Stephen says he has been produced by "This race and this country and this life," so can this be said of his father. It is in this way, and in the image of his own father, that we can realize how Stephen carries a sense of Ireland's history in his own consciousness. And at the same time he feels that he is a foreigner in Dublin, a foreigner in the sense that he is even forced to speak a language not his own. Just before his discussion of esthetics with the Jesuit dean of studies, Stephen realizes that "The Ireland of Tone and of Parnell seemed to have receded in space." He, Stephen, living in the Ireland after their failure, thinks, while talking to the dean: "I cannot speak or write these words without unrest of spirit. His language [the dean's], so familiar and so foreign, will always be for me an acquired speech. I have not made or accepted its words. My voice holds them at bay. My soul frets in the shadow of his language." Stephen's thoughts are highly suggestive, highly important, for an interpretation of this novel. When Joyce walked the streets of Dublin as a youth, one can be sure he constantly sensed the presence of the English in the major city of Ireland. One can speculate by asking how many little incidents, words, gestures, angers, glances of suspicion did he not grasp on the wing, all deepening a sense of the life of Dublin as a painful burden? The failure of the Irish to follow men like Tone and Parnell, meant that he, Stephen, must fret in speaking a language not his own. Again, it is revealed how Irish history presses on Stephen as something concrete, immediate, as a condition of life that affects him, threatens him with paralysis of soul. Such being the case, it should be clear as to why Joyce could find no inspiration in a cultural renaissance that found so much of theme and subject in a legendary Irish past. A real Irish presence was far, far too disturbing. Herein is the meaning of a remark Stephen utters in his own defense: "I am not responsible for the past." But, to repeat, he has seen the consequences of that past all about him in the present.

And since this is the case, Joyce is not going to find literary inspiration where the leading literary men of the time found it. He does not have to discover Ireland. He carries too much of it already in his own being.

—James T. Farrell, "Joyce's *A Portrait of the Artist as a Young Man*," (1944; reprint in *The League of Frightened Philistines and Other Papers*, New York: Vanguard, 1945), pp. 49–51

HUGH KENNER ON THE OPENING PAGES OF *A PORTRAIT OF THE ARTIST* AS PLOT METAPHOR

[Hugh Kenner (b. 1923) is a literary critic and the Andrew W. Mellon Professor of the Humanities at Johns Hopkins University. Kenner's publications include *Paradox in Chesterton* (1947), *The Poetry of Ezra Pound* (1985), and *Wyndham Lewis* (1954). In the following extract, taken from *Dublin's Joyce* (1955), Kenner views the opening of *A Portrait of the Artist* as an extended metaphor for Stephen's growth as an artist.]

According to the practice inaugurated by Joyce when he rewrote "The Sisters" in 1906, the *Portrait*, ⟨. . . .⟩ opens amid elaborate counterpoint. The first two pages, terminating in a row of asterisks, enact the entire action in microcosm. An Aristotelian catalogue of senses, faculties, and mental activities is played against the unfolding of the infant conscience ⟨. . . .⟩ This evocation of holes in oblivion is conducted in the mode of each of the five senses in turn; hearing (the story of the moocow), sight (his father's face), taste (lemon platt), touch (warm and cold), smell (the oil-sheet). The audible soothes: the visible disturbs. Throughout Joyce's work, the senses are symbolically disposed. Smell is the means of discriminating empirical realities ("His mother had a nicer smell than his father" is the next sentence), sight corresponds to the phantasms of oppression, hearing to the imaginative life. Touch and taste together are the modes of sex. Hearing, here, comes first, via a piece of imaginative literature ⟨. . . .⟩

[Stephen's d]awning consciousness of his own identity ("He was a baby tuckoo") leads to artistic performance ("He sang that song. That was his song.") This is hugely expanded in chapter IV:

> Now, as never before, his strange name seemed to him a prophecy . . . of the end he had been born to serve and had been following through the mists of childhood and boyhood, a symbol of the artist forging anew in his workshop out of the sluggish matter of the earth a new soaring impalpable imperishable being.

By changing the red rose to a green and dislocating the spelling, he makes the song his own ("But you could not have a green rose. But perhaps somewhere in the world you could.") ⟨. . . .⟩ the overture ends with Stephen hiding under the table awaiting the eagles. He is hiding under something most of the time: bedclothes, "the enigma of a manner," an indurated rhetoric, or some other carapace of his private world.

—Hugh Kenner, *Dublin's Joyce* (London: Chatto & Windus, 1955), pp. 114, 115–16

RICHARD ELLMANN ON EXILE AS ARTISTIC FREEDOM IN *A PORTRAIT OF THE ARTIST AS A YOUNG MAN*

[Richard Ellman (1918-1987), the renowned biographer and literary critic, lectured at Harvard University, Yale University, the University of Oxford, and the University of Chicago. He is the author of *Yeats: The Man and the Masks* (1948), *The Identity of Yeats* (1954), and *Oscar Wilde* (1987). His monumental work, *James Joyce* (1959), changed the way many scholars viewed the art of biography. In the following extract, Ellman comments on exile and artistic freedom in *A Portrait of the Artist*.]

Revolutionaries fatten on opposition but grow thin and pale when treated with indulgence. Joyce's ostracism from Dublin lacked, as he was well aware, the moral decisiveness of Dante's exile from Florence in that Joyce kept the keys to the gate. He was neither bidden to leave nor forbidden to return, and he did in fact go back four times. But whenever his relations with his native land seemed in danger of improving, he found a new incident to solidify his intransigence and reaffirm the rightness of his voluntary exile. He even showed some grand resentment at the possibility of Irish independence on the grounds that it would change the relationship he had so carefully established between himself and his country. "Should I," he asked someone, "wish to alter the conditions that have made me what I am?" At first he thought only his soul was in danger in Ireland. Then, when his difficulties over the publication of *Dubliners* became so great, he thought his writing career was being deliberately conspired against. Finally he came to assert that he was physically in danger. This suspicion began when his wife paid a visit to Galway in 1922. Civil war had just broken out in the west, and her train was fired on by soldiers. Joyce chose to believe that the bullets were really aimed at him, and afterwards refused to return to Ireland because he said he feared for his life. That Joyce could not have written his books in Ireland is likely enough, but he felt the need for maintaining his intimacy with his country by continually renewing the quarrel with her which prompted his first departure.

In his books too his heroes are outcasts in one way or another, and much of their interest lies in why they are cast out and by whom. Are they "self-doomed," as Joyce says of himself in his broadside, "The Holy Office," or are they doomed by society? To the extent that the hero is himself responsible, he is Faust-like, struggling like Stephen Dedalus or Richard Rowan to achieve a freedom beyond human power. To the extent that society is responsible he is Christlike, a sacrificial victim whose sufferings torment his tormentors. Joyce was not so masochistic as to identify completely with the helpless victim; at the very moment he attacks society most bitterly as his oppressor, he will not completely deny the authorship of his own despair. Like the boy in the ballad of the Jew's daughter, he is immolated, *consenting*. Again he was not so possessed with self as to adopt utterly the part of the anarchic individual. He carefully avoids making his heroes anything but unhappy in their triumphant self-righteousness.

Half-willing and half-forced to be a sufferer, Stephen endows the artist in *A Portrait of the Artist as a Young Man* with a rather similar mixture of qualities, the total power of a god bored by his own handiwork and the heroic impotence of a Lucifer, smarting from pain which he has chosen to bear. To be both god and devil is perhaps to be man. In *Ulysses* the paradoxes ascribed to these forces are the paradoxes of being Joyce: God begets Himself, sends himself between Himself and others, is put upon by His own friends. Joyce and Stephen challenge in the same way the forces which they have brought into being. As Stephen says of Shakespeare, "His unremitting intellect is the hornmad Iago ceaselessly willing that the moor in him shall suffer." If the residents of heaven were not androgynous, he says, God would be bawd and cuckold too, arranging for his own humiliation with his own creatures.

In his books Joyce represents heroes who seek freedom, which is also exile, voluntarily and by compulsion. The question of ultimate responsibility is raised and then dropped without an answer. Joyce's hero is as lonely as Byron's; consequently Joyce obliterated Stephen's brother, Maurice, from the *Portrait* after using him tentatively in *Stephen Hero*, for there must be no adherent, and the home must be a rallying-point of betrayal. A cluster of themes—the sacrilege of Faust, the suffering of Christ, the exile of Dante—reach a focus in the problem of friendship. For if friendship exists, it impugns the quality of exile and lonely heroism. If the world is not altogether hostile, we may forgive it for having mistreated us, and so be forced into the false position of warriors without adversaries. Joyce allows his hero to sample friendship before discovering its flaws, and then with the theme of broken friendship represents his hero's broken ties with Ireland and the world.

—Richard Ellman, "A Portrait of the Artist as Friend," *The Kenyon Review* 18, No. 1 (Winter 19): pp. 53–55

ANTHONY BURGESS ON THE FLIGHTS OF STEPHEN DEDALUS

[Anthony Burgess (b. 1917) is perhaps best known for his novel *A Clockwork Orange* (1962). He has also composed many orchestral works and has written several screenplays and television scripts, as well as a biography of Shakespeare (1970), and many articles on James Joyce. In the following extract, taken from *RE Joyce* (1965), Burgess explores the central symbol of *A Portrait of the Artist as a Young Man*—a creature learning to fly.]

A Portrait of the Artist as a Young Man has many symbols, but the fundamental one is of a creature trying to escape from the bondage of the grosser elements, earth and water, and learning painfully how to fly. The first of the five big chapters into which the book is organised begins with a child's discrete impressions—the father's fairy tale (the father comes first), the stumbling of an infant's tongue that is not yet a poet's, so that "O, the wild rose blossoms" becomes "O, the green wothe botheth," the smells of bed and father and mother, water. The embryonic soul is surrounded by a sort of amniotic fluid—urine and the sea (Stephen dances a hornpipe); as for the land, it has two colours—red and green. These are also heraldic or political colours: "Dante had two brushes in her press. The brush with the maroon velvet back was for Michael Davitt and the brush with the green velvet back was for Parnell." But the embryo is better used to darkness, and so Stephen hides under the table. Dante (Mrs. Riordan, his nurse) foretells his future,

> . . . His mother said:
> —O, Stephen will apologise.
> Dante said:
> —O, if not, the eagles will come and pull out his eyes—
>> Pull out his eyes,
>> Apologise,
>> Apologise,
>> Pull out his eyes.

The eagle, not the wren, is still the king of all birds, but he knows who is threatening to usurp his eyrie and he counter-threatens the poet with blindness.

This opening page is a swift miracle, the sort of achievement which, in its immediacy and astonishing economy, ought to make the conventional novelist ("My first memories are of my father, a monocled hirsute man who told me stories") ashamed. Prose and subject-matter have become one and inseparable; it is the first big technical breakthrough of twentieth-century prose-writing and, inevitably, it looks as if anybody could have thought of it. The roots of *Ulysses* are here—to every phrase of the soul its own special language; *Finnegans Wake* must seem, not a wilful aberration from sense, but a logical conclusion from that premise. If we recognize the rightness of "When you wet the bed first it is warm then it gets cold. His mother put on the oilsheet. That had the queer smell," we must accept the inevitability of "Till thousendsthee. Lps. The keys to. Given! A way a lone a last a loved a long the."

The section that follows takes Stephen to Clongowes Wood College. He is still a child, a creature of responses and not of thought, and he tries to hide from the boisterous world. The eye-pecking eagle has become a football: "the greasy leather orb flew like a heavy bird through the grey light." In the pale and chilly evening air he feels "his body small and weak amid the throng of players"; his eyes are "weak and watery." He is surrounded by mud and cold but he is also ill: a boy called Wells (appropriate name) shouldered him into the slimy water of the square ditch because he would not swap his snuffbox for a hacking chestnut. The soul is kept pushed down to its primal water and earth. Stephen hears one boy call another a "suck" and at once he hears and sees water going down a lavatory basin. The colours of the earth assert themselves: ". . . he remembered the song about the wild rose blossoms on the little green place. But you could not have a green rose. But perhaps somewhere in the world you could." A class-mate, Fleming, has coloured the earth and clouds on the first page of the geography book—the earth green and the clouds maroon. We are back to Dante's brushes and—gross forces which will try to hold the emergent soul to a particular spot on earth—Irish politics. Parnell is in Stephen's mind as he shivers in the study hall:

> He wondered which was right, to be for the green or the maroon, because Dante had ripped the green velvet back off the brush that was for Parnell one day with her scissors and had told him that Parnell was a bad man. He wondered if they were arguing at home about that. That was called politics. There were two sides in it: Dante was on one side and his father and Mr. Casey were on the other side but his mother and Uncle Charles were on no side.

When he is taken off to the school infirmary and his soul almost resigns itself to the earth ("How beautiful the words were where they said *Bury me in the old churchyard*!") he has a watery vision, full of the noise of waves, with the cry "Parnell! He is dead!" coming up from the crowd by the sea's edge. Dante, in maroon and green velvet, walks proudly and silently past.

—Anthony Burgess, *RE Joyce* (New York: W. W. Norton, 1965), pp. 50–51

❖

EVERT SPRINCHORN ON JOYCE AS SYMBOLIST

[Evert Sprinchorn (b. 1923), a professor of Drama at Vassar College, is also an editor and translator of the works of Swedish playwright August Strindberg. In the following extract, Sprinchorn asserts that a full understanding of *A Portrait of the Artist* requires an "intimate knowledge" of Christian lore, Greek myth, and other symbolist systems.]

Perhaps everyone who reads the *Portrait* for the first time puts the book down with a sense of disappointment arising from the last chapter. There one finds that the autobiographical hero Stephen Dedalus has been transformed from a sensitive boy into an apparently insensitive, insufferable, and "indigestibly Byronic" young man. How can one explain this change except by assuming, as some critics do, that Joyce intended to show his hero as an egotistic youth who will shortly get his comeuppance? And yet I wonder if this view does not offend the deepest instincts of every reader. During four of the five chapters in the book, the reader follows with great sympathy the attempts of Stephen to discover himself as an artist and to assert himself as a human being in a world where he has lived only a shadowy existence because he is half-blind, oversensitive, physically weak, and unhappy in love. At the end of the fourth chapter, in the memorable scene by the seashore, the miracle happens: Stephen is transformed. Is it at all likely that Joyce would have constructed his novel so that the regeneration of the sympathetic hero would be followed by his decline into a priggishness and egotism that alienates the reader from him? Aware that Joyce would scarcely have undercut his novel to this extent, the critics who think Stephen is insufferable have sought to detach the fifth chapter and to regard it as a separate work, different in tone and treatment from the others and serving as a bridge to *Ulysses*. However, Chapter V is Chapter V, and what we wish to know first of all is how it follows from the previous four chapters, not how it anticipates another work. And what we wish to understand finally is how Stephen becomes an artist, not an insufferable young man with a chip on his shoulder.

In order to reveal to a select few the secret of the making of a dedicated artist, while at the same time concealing that secret to the insensitive, and uncomprehending multitude, Joyce made use of all the characteristic techniques of the nineteenth-century symbolist, investing naturalistic detail with significance, implicitly comparing his characters to mythological, historical, and literary figures, transforming his symbols one into another in accordance with changes in mood or in point of view, minimizing external action in order to observe the movements of the soul, and constructing his work so that the relation of part to part conveys more meaning than what the hero does or thinks. The *Portrait*, not *Ulysses*, is the first novel in which Joyce perfected these techniques. One need only compare *Stephen Hero*, the early draft of the novel, with the finished *Portrait* to appreciate the extent to which Joyce reshaped the factual, autobiographical material in accordance with symbolist principles. The *Portrait* cannot be read like an ordinary novel any more than *Ulysses* can. To get at the heart of this novel, and to appreciate fully the brilliant technical achievement represented by the fifth chapter, Joyce expects his ideal reader to pay minute attention to detail and to have an intimate knowledge of Christian lore, Greek myth, obscure initiation mysteries, and nineteenth-century literature.

In no other work is Joyce so secretive as this, his most personal and most intimate work. It is significant that he never offered to help his readers with a key to the novel; he did not even provide an allusive title to hint that they should look for a key or that here was something more than the conventional *Bildungsroman*. Yet the secret of the artist lies there, buried in its quiet, dark depths, depths where the soul of an artist "has a slow and dark birth, more mysterious than the birth of the body."

—Evert Sprinchorn, "A Portrait of the Artist as Achilles," *Approaches to the Twentieth-Century Novel*, ed. John Unterecker (New York: Thomas Y. Crowell, 1965), pp. 9–11

A. WALTON LITZ ON LANGUAGE AS STRUCTURE IN *A PORTRAIT OF THE ARTIST*

[A. Walton Litz (b. 1929), a former professor of English and Chairman of the English Department of Princeton University, is also a prolific literary critic. Among his publications are *Modern American Fiction* (1963), *Jane Austen* (1965), and *Eliot and His Time* (1973). In the following extract, taken from *James Joyce* (1966), Litz argues that the power of Joyce's novel rests primarily with the "precise correlation of action and language."]

The complex structural analogies which unify *Portrait* are ⟨. . .⟩ dependent upon a highly charged symbolic language. Joyce's selective method precludes conventional transitions; we are presented with a number of crucial episodes in Stephen's life and are asked to infer the total pattern of his development from these separate episodes. As in T. S. Eliot's *The Waste Land*, the connections and transitions are suggested, not stated. This narrative technique places a much greater burden upon language than the conventional method of *Stephen Hero*. Each episode must be so freighted with symbolic significance that we can judge the whole from the part; the guiding metaphors form the backbone of the novel.

Typical of these guiding metaphors is the novel's complex water imagery. The first reference to water occurs in the fifth paragraph of *Portrait*. "When you wet the bed, first it is warm and then it gets cold." Already the image has two potentials, pleasurable and unpleasant. Later at school the word "suck" reminds Stephen of this twin potential: "To remember that and the white look of the lavatory made him feel cold and then hot. There were two cocks that you turned and water came out: cold and hot. He felt cold and then a little hot: and he could see the names printed on the cocks. That was a very queer thing."

Throughout most of Chapter One water has unpleasant associations. The bogwater of the Clongowes baths disgusts Stephen; Wells shoulders him into the "cold and slimy" water of the square ditch. The vision of death comes to him across a sea of waves. But at the end of the chapter, after Stephen's apparent victory over Father Dolan, water suddenly takes on a new and pleasing significance. "The fellows were practising long shies and bowling lobs and slow twisters. In the soft grey silence he could hear the bump of the balls: and from here and from there through the quiet air the sound of the cricket bats: pick, pack, pock, puck: like drops of water in a fountain falling softly in the brimming bowl." As Stephen's state of mind has changed, so have the emotions suggested by water. The final image of drops falling softly into a brimming fountain brings Chapter One to a close on a theme of purification which carries with it overtones of baptism.

Thus in the first chapter of *Portrait* Joyce establishes a twin symbolism of birth and death. Like Eliot in *The Waste Land*, he is exploiting the ambivalence of our traditional associations with water (drowning and baptism). Depending upon the context, water imagery in the *Portrait* may point toward either pleasure or. pain, life or death; or it may be used to suggest both at once. Stephen fears the sea since he views it as an emblem of his own futility; but ironically it is the seaside epiphany whuch awakens him to the demands of life. Toward the end of Chapter Four the water symbolism becomes more subtle, more complex, until all its potentialities are exploited in the final scene of that chapter.

Yet we must remember that the repeated references to water make up only one of many chains of imagery which sew the novel together from the inside. Joyce's descriptive language is charged at every point with symbolic significance, and it is this constant use of symbolism which enables him to convey a full impression of Stephen's development through a few carefully selected episodes. Each episode is not merely an event in Stephen's life, but an epiphany of one aspect of his personality.

Another characteristic of the *Portrait*'s language which should be noted in passing is the manner in which the style changes as Stephen grows toward maturity. Generally speaking, the movement of the novel is from subjective identification with the young Stephen Dedalus to a dramatic presentation of the adolescent artist. In the first chapter Joyce's language almost forces us to identify ourselves with Stephen, yet by the time we reach Chapter Five the style has become so dispassionate that we are able to stand apart from Stephen and judge his actions.

But this general movement from lyrical to dramatic, from subjective to objective treatment, is not the only pattern to be noted. Within this general movement we can discern smaller oscillations between the lyrical and dramatic styles which correspond to those in Stephen's fortune. Each chapter ends on a tone of intense lyricism, corresponding to Stephen's new-found hope; but then—as we move into the next chapter—there is an abrupt change in language which reflects the decline in Stephen's resolution. Thus the splendid lyrical close to Chapter Four, which expresses Stephen's ecstatic acceptance of life, is immediately undercut at the beginning of Chapter Five by the sordid description of Stephen's home. Chapter Four ends with the turning of the tide and a few reflections in distant pools of water—all is serene and calm, the water serving as an emblem of new life. But the next paragraph, which opens Chapter Five, exploits the antithetical value of water: "He drained his third cup of watery tea to the dregs and set to chewing the crusts of fried bread that were scattered near him, staring into the dark pool of the jar. The yellow dripping had been scooped out like a boghole, and the pool under it brought back to his memory the dark turfcoloured water of the bath in Clongowes." Here the tone of the language has been radically changed, the symbolism reversed, and this abrupt reversal emphasizes the change in Stephen's state of mind. *A Portrait of the Artist as a Young Man* owes much of its extraordinary impact to Joyce's precise correlation of action and language.

—A. Walton Litz, *James Joyce* (New York: Twayne Publishers, 1966), pp. 67–69

C. H. Peake on Stephen Dedalus and Emma

[C. H. Peake (c. 1920–1988) was an important Joyce scholar and wrote a number of works on Jonathan Swift. He also edited *Poetry of Landscape and the Night: Two Eighteenth-Century Traditions* (1967). In the following extract, taken from *James Joyce: The Citizen and the Artist* (1977), Peake views Stephen Dedalus's attempt to detach himself from Emma as the final step in his "struggle for isolation."]

⟨. . . .⟩ Emma is for Stephen a female body in which his imagination can locate the sexual appeal of the prostitute, the spiritual uplift of the Virgin and the rhapsodic inspiration of the Muse-girl on the shore. But besides serving to provide a bodily form for Stephen's dreams, she is also the chief threat to his assumed detachment. He fluctuates between desire and loathing, until, like the boy in "Araby," he sees all his highflown dreams of her as vanities. Because so many of his enfeebling dreams have been incarnate for him in the figure of the girl, his perception of the self-deceit which has characterized his feelings towards her serves as a more general self-liberation, and, as this illusion has been represented by the posturing poeticism of the "Villanelle" [in *Stephen Hero*], so the act of liberation is prompted by a critical recognition, in his next encounter with the girl, of the falseness of this poetic abandonment.

She passes, and the air seems silent after her passage: he thinks of the line, *"Darkness falls from the air,"* and, moved by "a trembling joy," is unsure whether it is her passing or the beauty of the verse which has so moved him. But the verse evokes the Stuart period and with it the sexual squalor beneath the musical and verbal grace of that time—an historical projection of his own physical desire concealed behind poetical and spiritual disguises. He checks himself lest her image be contaminated:

> That was not the way to think of her. It was not even the way in which he thought of her. Could his mind then not trust itself?

At once he imagines her passing homewards, and senses the smell of her body and her underclothes, "a wild and languid smell." The wildness and languor of the "Villanelle" has been metamorphosed from spirit to matter. A louse crawling on his neck disturbs him; he suddenly remembers that Nash's line was "*Brightness falls from the air*," and all the images prompted by the misquoted line are seen to have been false: "His mind bred vermin. His thoughts were lice born of the sweat of sloth." The revulsion, following this new perception of his vanity, is such that he decides to "let her go and be damned to her. She could love some clean athlete who washed himself every morning to the waist and had black hair on his chest. Let her."

This curious and involved revolution of attitude is not to be explained in logical terms; but some concatenative mental process is clearly at work. The association of the girl with the misquoted line of verse is part of the habitual poetic aura with which Stephen clothes his feelings towards her, but as a consequence of the sexual images produced by the historical and literary associations of the line (although he denies they have any reference to the girl) "a conscious unrest seethed in his blood" and an unmistakably physical and sexual desire awakes, focused not on the customary Swinburnian image of nakedness but on the smell of her body "and the secret soft linen upon which her flesh distilled odour and a dew." The combination of this poetical perspiration and the appearance of the louse recalls the old superstition that lice were born of human sweat, and induces the image of his own body "illclad, illfed, louseeaten." ⟨. . . .⟩ The revulsion is not due to a horrified perception that Emma's body-odours and his lice-breeding sweat are the same, but rather to the realization that the fantasy he has made of the girl is merely a slothful exudation of his mind, disguising physical desire as poetic devotion. ⟨. . . .⟩ Once the true nature of his feelings emerges from the "cloudy circumstance" and rosy afterglow in which his poem was conceived, once the "wilful heart" and "look of languor" of the dream image have been transmuted to "a wild and languid smell," the girl loses her hold on his imagination. Later, talking to Cranly, and perceiving that his friend would shield a woman and bow his mind to her, Stephen knows that his own feelings for the girl have no real place in his life: "He could not strive against another. He knew his part." His part, as artist, seems to him, at this stage, to keep out of the struggle, to detach himself, and the obsession with the girl is the last skin but one that he must strip off to be free. Later he writes in his diary that he is "soulfree and fancyfree," and adds, "And let the dead marry the dead. ⟨. . . .⟩ This is the confident assertion of the artist that his past is important only because it serves as the fuel of the present, making him what he is, and being destroyed (in its original form) in the process, while the only importance, for the potential artist, of what he is, is its contribution to what he will become and produce in the future.

—C. H. Peake, *James Joyce: The Citizen and the Artist* (Stanford, CA: Stanford University Press, 1977), pp. 80–82

JAMES CARENS ON THE MOTIF OF HANDS IN *A PORTRAIT OF THE ARTIST AS A YOUNG MAN*

[James Carens is an associate professor of English at Bucknell University and director of the Bucknell University Press. He is the author of *The Satiric Art of Evelyn Waugh* (1966) and *Surpassing Wit: Oliver St. John Gogarty, His Poetry and His Prose* (1979). In the following extract, Carens explores the motif of hands in *A Portrait of the Artist* as an example of the way in which the meanings of Joyce's symbols shift according to context.]

It was characteristic of Joyce in *Portrait* and elsewhere to develop his motifs by accretion of detail and amplification of suggested meanings. The values and connotations of his metaphors, his images, and his motifs are seldom fixed; symbolic overtones emerge from particular contexts; they then adhere to a motif as it is carried into a new context. There are, for instance, clusters of hand references in chapter 3 and later in the novel which, even if we artificially dissociate them from what has gone before, do take on symbolic overtones. When Joyce begins his account of the religious retreat that fills Stephen with loathing and disgust for his life of sexual debauchery, he draws attention to the rector's hands, "clasped . . . on the desk"; in the midst of his announcement, the rector is described as "shaking his clasped hands before him"; finally, his announcement over, "he ceased to shake his clasped hands and, resting them against his forehead, looked right and left of them keenly at his listeners out of his dark stern eyes." In truth, the apparent gesture of piety is an oratorical device calculated to influence the rector's audience, as is the stern glance that he casts at them. Ironically enough, then, when Stephen, hysterical with guilt and the desire to confess, later seeks some chapel in a remote part of Dublin, he is directed to Church Street chapel by an old woman who holds "out her reeking withered right hand." The boy who had been repelled by Mike Flynn's swollen stained fingers bends "lower towards her, saddened and soothed by her voice." When he is in the chapel, Stephen bows "his head upon his hands," and then, kneeling before the crucifix in the confessional, he clasps his hands and raises them "towards the white form." The following morning his hands and soul tremble as he takes communion. Not only is Stephen duplicating the contrived gesture of the rector when he clasps his hands, but he is submitting to the terror and repression that had made his body shake with fear years before when his hands were struck with a pandybat at Clongowes. Each of the allusions to clasped or praying hands carries an implication of repression and inversion. Thus when, early in chapter 4, Stephen apes the essentially erotic "attitude of rapture in sacred art, the raised and parted hands, the parted lips and eyes as of one about to swoon," we know that he will not long be able to continue his repressive behavior. In short, such hand allusions as these I have cited may be taken as an element in the verisimilitude of the fiction, but they also imply emotional and moral significances within a particular context, and their meanings are further enlarged by the details of a motif that has already been developed into a complex of implications.

—James Carens, "The Motif of Hands in *A Portrait of the Artist as a Young Man*," *Irish Renaissance Annual II*, ed. Zack Bowen (Newark, DE: University of Delaware Press, 1981), pp. 141–42

Martin Price on Stephen Dedalus's Conception of Art and the Artist

[Martin Price, (b. 1920) an editor, author, and critic, is also Sterling Professor of English at Yale University. His publications include *Swift's Rhetorical Art: A Study in Structure and Meaning* (1953). In the following extract, taken from *Forms of Life: Character and Moral Imagination in the Novel* (1983), Price examines Stephen Dedalus's development as an artist in light of his complete rejection of the duties of "practical life."]

In the final chapter of [*A Portrait of the Artist as a Young Man*], Joyce sets forth the claims upon Stephen of both church and nation and meets them with the vocation of the artist. Ireland has become a constellation of demands and affronts, and Stephen sees its debasement in the statue of Tom Moore, the "national poet": "He looked at it without anger: for, though sloth of the body and of the soul crept over it like unseen vermin, over the shuffling feet and up the folds of the cloak and around the servile head, it seemed humbly unconscious of its indignity." Stephen is reminded of Davin, "the peasant student," "one of the tame geese," regarding Ireland with the same uncritical acceptance he shows for the Roman Catholic religion, "the attitude of a dullwitted loyal serf." Davin in turn evokes the Irish peasant woman who invited him to her bed, a "type of her race and his own, a bat-like soul waking to the consciousness of itself in darkness and secrecy and loneliness." At every point Stephen opposes the Irish scene with associations that come from elsewhere—Newman, Cavalcanti, Ibsen, Jonson. "Try to be one of us," Davin asks. "In your heart you are an Irishman but your pride is too powerful." But Stephen must see Ireland's claims as captivity: "When the soul of a man is born in this country there are nets flung at it to hold it back from flight. You talk to me of nationality, language, religion. I shall try to fly by those nets." He parries the claims that his friend Cranly advances in Ireland's behalf, the most compelling of them Stephen's mother's wish that he remain in the faith. "Whatever she feels, it, at least, must be real," Cranly insists. "It must be. What are our ideas or ambitions? Play.

Ideas!" Cranly asserts that Stephen has more religious faith than he knows, that his doubts are only an expression of that faith. And it is through his replies to Cranly that Stephen extricates himself from all the claims made upon him: "I will not serve that in which I no longer believe whether it call itself my home, my fatherland or my church: and I will try to express myself in some mode of life or art as freely as I can and as wholly as I can, using for my defence the only arms I allow myself to use—silence, exile, and cunning."

The aesthetic Stephen formulates is a culmination of this movement toward freedom. It is not an assertion of the purity of art but of its autonomy. Out of the natural feelings there emerges a peculiar "aesthetic emotion," not so much a distinct kind as a distinct form of emotion. The feelings of practical life—kinetic, concerned with possession or avoidance but in either case with motion—undergo an "arrest."

It is in such moments of arrest that we enter a "mental world." We are beyond the "purely reflex action of the nervous system" and reach a realm of free contemplation, an "esthetic stasis" in which we feel no excitation to action, but rather "an ideal pity or an ideal terror." This stasis is experience framed, discontinuous with the stream of ordinary feelings; the framing is achieved by aesthetic form—"the rhythm of beauty." Stephen states the freedom of the aesthetic response with mock-solemnity: we "try slowly and humbly and constantly to express, to press out again, from the gross earth or what it brings forth [Lynch has amiably protested, "please remember, though I did eat a cake of cowdung once, that I admire only beauty"], from sound and shape and colour which are the prison gates of our soul, an image of the beauty we have come to understand—that is art." Stephen (and certainly Joyce) is too much the Aristotelian to speak of the objects of the senses as the "prison gates of our soul" except with a certain ironic exaggeration. He is perhaps stirred by Lynch's grossness to insist upon the cognitive, upon an intellectual beauty that contrasts with sensory impressions. But as he speaks, the novelist insists in turn upon the concreteness of the physical world: "They had reached the canal bridge and, turning from their course, went on by the trees. A crude grey light, mirrored in the sluggish water, and a smell of wet branches over their heads seemed to war against the course of Stephen's thought."

Stephen's definition of art includes the senses as much as the intellect: it is "the human disposition of sensible or intelligible matter for an esthetic end." What matters is that both are liberated from the practical, the moral, the kinetic; if the immediate object of beauty is pleasure, it remains indifferent to judgments of good and evil. Stephen is freeing the work of art as he is freeing himself from the claims that are being pressed upon both—duty to church and to country. The aesthetic becomes a privileged experience: it has autonomy within its own province, and it has the duty to itself, as it were, of becoming a work of art, just as Stephen owes himself the initial duty of becoming an artist.

—Martin Price, *Forms of Life: Character and Moral Imagination in the Novel* (New Haven: Yale University Press, 1983), pp. 316–17

PATRICK PARRINDER ON *A PORTRAIT OF THE ARTIST* AS *BILDUNGSROMAN*

[Patrick Parrinder, (b. 1949) a literary critic and author, is a professor of English at the University of Reading in England. He is the author of *H. G. Wells* (1970), *Authors and Authority* (1977), and *The Failure of Theory* (1987). In the following extract, taken from *James Joyce* (1984), Parrinder compares Joyce's *A Portrait of the Artist as a Young Man* to the memoirs and *Bildungsromane* ("novels of education") of nineteenth-century authors.]

Joyce started off, as few if any novelists before him had done, by sticking scrupulously to the ostensible facts of his own life. His rewriting of the main events of his life is as nothing compared with the melodramatic inventions to be found in even the most "confessional" of earlier novels. This is the main point of difference between the *Portrait* and *Bildungsromane* and *Künstlerromane* ("novels of education" and "artist-hero" novels) of the nineteenth century. The *Portrait* is less close to books like *Wilhelm Meister, David Copperfield,* or Gissing's *New Grub Street* than it is to the genre of literary autobiography and memoirs. The pattern of destiny which Stephen discovers in the events of his own life suggests that one crucial source is the tradition of spiritual apology or confession, from St. Augustine to Newman. Stephen's destiny, however, bears witness to the religion of Art rather than of Christianity, and it is in the field of artistic memoirs and autobiographical sketches that we shall find the closest analogues to the *Portrait*. One such memoir by an older contemporary—George Moore's *Confessions of a Young Man* (1888)—no doubt influenced Joyce's title.

Stephen's belief in the priestly role of the artist and his duty to "forge in the smithy of my soul the uncreated conscience of my race" has its roots in the high romanticism of Wordsworth and Shelley. The *Portrait* transmutes the stuff of actual experience into artistic myth as thoroughly as Wordsworth had done. In addition, it serves as a "prelude" in the Wordsworthian sense to the more comprehensive edifices of *Ulysses* and *Finnegans Wake*. Nevertheless, the *Portrait* is not a straightforwardly romantic work. While Stephen remains ultimately committed to the Shelleyan notion of the artist as unacknowledged legislator of the world, his attention—unlike that of the Wordsworthian or Shelleyan hero—is devoted to disentangling himself from the external world and exploring the secrets and intricacies of his own art. His preoccupation with art as a sacred mystery links him to the Aesthetic and Decadent movements of the late nineteenth century. The reverence that the Aesthetes and Decadents felt for their romantic predecessors was tinged by the melancholy conviction that these poets had sought in the external world for "what is there in no satisfying measure or not at all." (These words, borrowed from Walter Pater, were used by Joyce himself in his essay on the Dublin romantic poet James Clarence Mangan.) The artist now turned, not to unspoilt nature, but in on himself to find a truly satisfying richness and beauty. Oscar Wilde went so far as to suggest that all artists are solipsists, whether they know it or not: "every portrait that is painted with feeling is a portrait of the artist," we read in *The Picture of Dorian Gray*. It may have been a similar conviction that led Joyce to turn to autobiographical fiction in the first place.

Stephen Hero is written in the naturalistic manner and portrays Stephen, during his student years, as an Ibsenite. Early in 1904, however, Joyce had written a short essay called "A Portrait of the Artist" which contrasts sharply with *Stephen Hero* even though Joyce incorporated some passages from it into his novel. The "Portrait of the Artist" was—understandably—rejected by the editors of *Dana* as incomprehensible. Far from presenting the artist as a free-standing fictional character, through realistic description and dramatized dialogue, Joyce had written a tortuous, allusive and contemplative essay modelled on the Walter Pater of *Imaginary Portraits* (1887). Such a portrait was, as he expressed it, "not an identificative paper but rather the curve of an emotion." The artist portrayed is one who turns aside from his contemporaries to seek the "image of beauty" in the byways of esoteric and occult learning. Though the essay concludes with a Shelleyan vision of social revolution, there is no suggestion here (as there was in the "epiphany" passage of *Stephen Hero*) that the artist might find beauty in the "commonest object" or amongst the people around him. Instead, "To those multitudes not as yet in the wombs of humanity but surely engenderable there, he would give the word."

—Patrick Parrinder, James Joyce (Cambridge: Cambridge University Press, 1984), pp. 72–73

JOSEPH A. BUTTIGIEG ON STEPHEN'S OBSTACLES TO BECOMING AN ARTIST

[Joseph A. Buttigieg is a Joyce scholar and author of *A Portrait of the Artist in Different Perspective* (1987), from which the following extract is taken. Buttigieg compares Stephen's attempt to escape history with the

necessity of developing new critical approaches to
Joyce's work.]

Stephen Dedalus recognizes early in his life the need to escape
the murderous burden placed upon him by a sacrosanct tradition. In both *A Portrait of the Artist as a Young Man* and *Ulysses*
we find him struggling against the nets which constrain him
and the ghosts that haunt him. In both novels Joyce traces the
progress of Stephen as he moves wilfully toward fulfilling his
self-imposed artistic vocation. Yet, it must be stressed, Joyce
never produces a picture of Stephen as creator but only of
Stephen in the throes of becoming a creator. Whatever Stephen
might think of himself, there should be little doubt that in *A
Portrait* and in *Ulysses* he is still struggling against those forces
which prevent him from attaining the status of a genuine, as
opposed to a self-styled, artist. The forces which campaign
against Stephen's emergence as artist, in the full Nietzschean
sense of creator, are the ghosts of history, the phantasms of his
own past as well as the phantasms foisted upon him by his
country and his religion. The two are hardly separable. Stephen
is not unaware of these ghosts nor is he blind to their pervasive
influence. He knows he has to free himself from the excess of
history in order to become the creator of a new order; "—
History, Stephen said, is a nightmare from which I am trying to
awake." Nevertheless, Stephen often fails to realize fully the
extent to which he is enmeshed in that nightmare, and consequently his declarations of freedom are, with possibly one
exception, premature. (The possible exception occurs when
Stephen smashes the lamp with his ashplant in the phantas-
magoric "Circe" chapter [of *Ulysses*].) There is one thing,
however, which Stephen thoroughly understands and about
which he is certain: in order to escape paralysis he must "bring
the past to the bar of judgement, interrogate it remorselessly,
and finally condemn it."

In our time, the conflict with the inherited tradition in
literary critical studies must likewise take the form of a
remorseless interrogation which should result in a *critical* (in
the Nietzschean sense) history of Modernism. The classics of
Modernism present the postmodern age with a problem not
entirely different from the one which for Pope and Dryden was

posed by the Greek and Roman classics—they threaten to become a debilitating force, they might induce paralysis. Hence, one of the most pressing needs of postmodernism is to produce a critical history, as opposed to a monumental history, of Modernism. The postmodern age must construct its own definition of Modernism. In a sense, of course, Modernism has already been defined and its monuments identified; but the prevailing definitions of Modernism and the privilege conferred upon certain texts deemed central to it come to us as part of that very same tradition which we must now confront critically and "interrogate remorselessly." For this reason, the construction of a postmodern definition of Modernism is inseparable from the "destruction" of the received tradition. "Destruction" here derives its special meaning from Martin Heidegger who, like Nietzsche, has made clear the problem that arises from the uncritical acceptance and transmission of tradition. "When tradition thus becomes master, it does so in such a way that what it 'transmits' is made so inaccessible, proximally and for the most part, that it rather becomes concealed. Tradition takes what has come down to us and delivers it over to self-evidence; it blocks our access to those primordial 'sources' from which the categories and concepts handed down to us have been in part quite genuinely drawn. Indeed it makes us forget that they have had such an origin. . . ." To overcome this forgetfulness Heidegger proposes the critical method of "destruction." As he hastens to make clear, "to bury the past in nullity . . . is not the purpose of this destruction; its aim is *positive*." Destruction enables the interpreter "to go back to the Past in a positive manner and make it productively his own." 〈. . . .〉

The importance of Joyce's texts in the Modernist pantheon is so great that any attempt to understand Modernism must include a careful consideration of Joyce's novels and the preeminent—one might even say paradigmatic or classic—status they enjoy. Yet, precisely because these texts are constitutive of Modernism as it has been habitually understood, it is especially difficult to examine them anew. They cannot be separated easily from the tradition which they both exemplify and constitute. It is quite hard to read them in a manner that differs significantly from the way in which they have already been read and presented. Still, any new beginning with regard to these texts must contend with the problem of extricating them from the authoritative critical and historical literary discourse that envelops them. In other words, if Joyce's *A Portrait of the Artist as a Young Man* and *Ulysses* are to be reappropriated for a postmodern readership, if they are not to be abandoned as the beautiful but ossified monuments of a dead past (i.e., a Modernism that once was and is no more), then their reappropriation will involve an analysis and critique of Modernism. Simultaneously, a critical or revisionary approach to Modernism necessarily entails a reconsideration of its canonical texts among which Joyce's novels occupy a very special place. These two tasks are one and the same and must be carried out concurrently because they cannot be separated effectively.

—Joseph A. Buttigieg, *A Portrait of the Artist in Different Perspective* (Athens, OH: Ohio University Press, 1987), pp. 10–12

JOHN BLADES ON MOMENTS OF EPIPHANY IN *A PORTRAIT OF THE ARTIST AS A YOUNG MAN*

[John Blades is the author of *James Joyce: A Portrait of the Artist as a Young Man* (1991), from which the following extract is taken. Blades explores Joyce's definition of "epiphany" as both a revelation of truth and a "heightened spiritual elation."]

Fundamental to an appreciation of Joyce's approach in *A Portrait* is an understanding of his concept of the "epiphany" and its use. As defined by Stephen and used by Joyce, it is crucially important not only to this novel but to all of Joyce's work, since in its implications it widely embraces the themes of time, truth, morality and art. However, *A Portrait* marks a step forward for Joyce's development as a writer in that, while all his previous work—*Chamber Music*, *Dubliners*, and *Stephen Hero*—also employs essentially isolated epiphanies held together in varying degrees of unity, *A Portrait* incorporates a sequence of related epiphanies in the form of a coherent narrative.

⟨. . .⟩ What exactly does Joyce mean by the word? For a formal definition of "epiphany" we must go outside *A Portrait* and to its earlier version, *Stephen Hero*, where Stephen, idly composing his "Villanelle of the Temptress" in Chapter XXV, overhears fragments of a conversation between two people:

> This triviality made him think of collecting many such moments together in a book of epiphanies. By an epiphany he meant a sudden spiritual manifestation, whether in the vulgarity of speech or of gesture or in a memorable phase of the mind itself. He believed that it was for the man of letters to record these epiphanies with extreme care, seeing that they themselves are the most delicate and evanescent of moments. He told Cranly that the clock of the Ballast Office was capable of an epiphany. Cranly questioned the inscrutable dial of the Ballast Office with his no less inscrutable countenance.
>
> —Yes, said Stephen. I will pass it time after time, allude to it, refer to it, catch a glimpse of it. It is only an item in the catalogue of Dublin's street furniture. Then all at once I see it and I know at once what it is: epiphany.
>
> —What?
>
> —Imagine my glimpses at that clock as the gropings of a spiritual eye which seeks to adjust its vision to an exact focus. The moment the focus is reached the object is epiphanized.
>
> (*Stephen Hero*)

Joyce, of course, borrows the term from the religious context—the feast day celebrating the revelation of the infant Christ to ordinary mortal mankind represented in the three Magi. Clearly, Joyce's concept takes up this idea of a manifestation—a showing forth of the reality of an object, a person, an event, etc. to the observer, with the suggestion also of privileged spiritual insight. Joyce discovered the phenomenon early in his teens, and Stanislaus [Joyce] in his biography records his brother's practice of collecting such moments:

> . . . manifestations or revelations . . . little errors and gestures—
> mere straws in the wind—by which people betrayed the very
> things they were most careful to conceal. "Epiphanies" were
> always brief sketches . . . (*My Brother's Keeper*)

In *Chamber Music*, almost every poem is centred on a single precise epiphany, presented with youthful reverence, while in *Dubliners*, each story consists of one or a number of epiphanies by which a character (and/or the reader) comes to realize the truth of his circumstances and the paralysing limitations of them. On the other hand, in *Ulysses*, an older, self-mocking Stephen scorns his own youthful reverence for epiphanies and his eager collecting of them, as he contemplates his languishing artistic ambitions:

> Remember your epiphanies written on green oval leaves, deeply
> deep, copies to be sent if you died to all the great libraries of the
> world, including Alexandria? Someone was to read them there
> after a few thousand years . . . (*Ulysses*)

In *A Portrait*, Joyce advances the use of epiphanies not only as a fundamentally significant literary technique but also as an important philosophical concept which was to become the cornerstone of his own mature works—and a cornerstone of Modernism in general.

In Stephen's definition and in Joyce's practice the term has two meanings: one is that an epiphany reveals the truth, the intrinsic essence of a person or of something which is observed, revealed perhaps through a "vulgarity of speech or of gesture"; and the second meaning is a state of mind, a heightened spiritual elation of the observer's mind, what Joyce calls the "memorable phase of the mind itself." The first puts emphasis on the object and the fact that its reality can be revealed by an epiphany, while the second puts emphasis on the observer, for whom an epiphany can be a state of spiritual ecstasy. Consequently, although we would normally think of the acquisition of knowledge in terms of a rational process, both of these meanings involve non-rational states, and insofar as they involve knowledge (either about an object or about oneself), the process implies a subjective source of truth, knowledge as a sort of intuition. In fact, as Stanislaus records, epiphanies can even include dreams—especially so since Joyce considered dreams to be a subconscious re-shaping or sharpening of everyday reality.

—John Blades, *James Joyce: A Portrait of the Artist as a Young Man* (London: Penguin Books, 1991), pp. 155–57

Patrick Colm Hogan on James Joyce and John Milton

[Patrick Colm Hogan (b. 1957) is an associate professor of English and Comparative Literature at the University of Connecticut. He is the author of *The Politics of Interpretation: Ideology, Professionalism, and the Study of Literature* (1990) and *Joyce, Milton, and the Theory of Influence* (1995), from which the following extract is taken. Hogan considers some biographical and literary similarities between James Joyce and John Milton.]

The most obvious personal connection linking Milton and Joyce is blindness. Though Joyce's sight was never fully lost, it was exceptionally poor from his youth, and like Milton's, declined rapidly in middle age. As [Matthew J. C.] Hodgart points out, in the *Wake* Joyce refers to his blindness in a Miltonic phrase that clearly links the sightlessness of these two Homeric poets. Joseph Schork has expanded Hodgart's observation, uncovering a larger complex of similar connections. But Milton went blind from excessive unillumined labors as Latin secretary for the Council of State, as an assiduous worker for a government that was notorious for its cruelty in the western colony of Ireland. Joyce went blind from poverty and drink.

The case is similar with the coat of arms. Joyce's somewhat pathetic concern with his coat of arms is well known. He found romance in the idea of a noble paternal past. Oddly, as Michael O'Shea points out, "the Joyce arms are remarkably similar to those of John Milton." It is hard to say whether Joyce knew the Milton coat of arms—or even, for that matter, the correct Joyce coat of arms. (The reproduction he owned, O'Shea explains, was faulty.) But given his remarkable interest in heraldry and its function in works such as *A Portrait* (as discussed by O'Shea), it is certainly not impossible. Again a noteworthy link, a connection encouraging identification. But the context impedes the identification. For Milton's coat of arms was "genuine" and meaningful. He was the conqueror, the propertied Sassenach. Joyce's coat of arms was a dubious attempt to uncover a shred of nobility behind squalor, an attempt without social or political consequence. Whatever Joyce's Norman ancestors may have been, he was now the conquered, ignoble Celt.

Other personal similarities are less starkly oppositional. For example, [George] Saintsbury (an author Joyce greatly admired) points out in his *Short History of English Literature* (owned by Joyce in Trieste) that the "only other member of the [Milton] family who is remembered was the poet's younger brother Christopher," a judge and a Royalist, in many ways the opposite of John. Not only is Stanislaus, James's younger brother and opposite, the only other member of the Joyce family who is remembered, [but] James must have been well aware from early on that this would be the case.

One of the best-known anecdotes about Milton's life provides a further connection. The elaborate treatment given by Joyce to Stephen's pandying by Father Dolan—not only in *A Portrait*, chapter 1, but in the "Circe" episode of *Ulysses* as well—is no doubt due in part to the powerful impression made on Joyce by a real incident of this sort in his own life. But it also recapitulates a famous incident in the life of Milton, when, as Samuel Johnson put it in his *Lives of the English Poets* (owned by Joyce in Trieste), Milton "suffered the public indignity of corporal correction" at school. Whether this event in Milton's life provided a selection principle for Joyce's writing is not so important here as the fact that when Joyce learned of Milton's punishment, he could hardly have avoided connecting it in his mind with his own humiliating experience.

A further and deeper similarity may be found in the fact that Milton, like Joyce, considered entering the clergy after leaving school. But like Joyce he ultimately decided against a religious life. Moreover, he came to this decision for the Joycean (that is,

Satanic, Miltonic) reason that he could not agree to obey, to "subscribe slave" as he put it (quoted in Johnson). As Johnson explains, "the thoughts of obedience, whether canonical or civil, raised his indignation." Milton might well have adopted Stephen's creed: "obedience" only "in the womb" (*Ulysses*).

Also like Joyce, Milton went to Italy after his mother's death and there developed his first serious poetic ambitions. Indeed, these ambitions and their relation to the sojourn in Italy are expounded in "The Reason of Church Government" in precisely the passage from which Joyce quotes in the "Pola" notebook and, subsequently, "The Dead." But, unlike Joyce, Milton's poetic ambitions were fired by literary success, and not by the oppression, censorship, and grinding poverty that Joyce suffered.

Finally, for some time after returning from Europe, Milton served as instructor "vapour[ing] away" his time in "a private boarding school" (Johnson), a fact to which Joyce alludes when he has Stephen, more than a year after returning from Europe, similarly vaporing away his time by teaching "Lycidas." Unlike Joyce, however, Milton left his teaching, not to travel again across the channel, but to take part in the turmoil that was then rending English society. Unlike Joyce, he set aside his poetic aspirations to engage himself politically—turning ultimately to a highly didactic art of precisely the sort Joyce denounced in "Drama and Life" (*Collected Works*), *A Portrait*, and elsewhere. The very fact that each had to make such a decision between politics and art, the fact that each wrote in a time of civil war and Anglo-Irish war, indicates that the similar soil claimed necessary by [Bjorn] Tysdahl was, to a degree, present. And yet, once again, the identities here are reversed like images in a mirror, oppositions as much as identifications, common properties rendered irreconcilable, for not only did Milton join in the political fray, he joined the enemy. And perhaps if Milton's side had not been victorious, however briefly, Joyce would never have been faced with a political decision. Perhaps the country into which he was born would not have been placed just beyond the margin of European civilization, Europe's odd European colony, and one of its most brutalized.

—Patrick Colm Hogan, *Joyce, Milton, and the Theory of Influence* (Gainesville, FL: University Press of Florida, 1995), pp. 60–62

David Glover on James Joyce and Popular Culture

[David Glover, a literary critic, is the author of an intriguing article, "A Tale of 'Unwashed Joyceans': James Joyce, Popular Culture, and Popular Theory," from which the following is extracted. Glover examines the general public's fascination with James Joyce as due in part to the evolution of popular culture itself.]

To invoke Joyce and popular culture in the same breath is inevitably to recognize that "cultural categories of high and low, social and aesthetic . . . are never entirely separable." And one reason for this has to do with the endlessly revisable character of cultural categories per se, which can never be settled once and for all. There is—as Peter Stallybrass and Allon White have suggested in their influential study *The Politics and Poetics of Transgression*—a "recurrent pattern" in the "mechanisms of ordering and sense-making in European cultures" in which "the 'top' attempts to reject or eliminate the 'bottom' for reasons of prestige and status." Yet ultimately high culture is bound to discover "not only that it is in some way dependent upon that low-Other . . . but also that the top *includes* that low symbolically, as a primary eroticized constituent of its own fantasy life." In a sense, one can read *A Portrait of the Artist as a Young Man* as a text whose credo of "silence, exile, and cunning" elegantly and guiltily engages with this ambivalent and deeply contradictory "fusion of power, fear and desire." However, it is the fluidity and instability of cultural boundaries and the consequences this has for the popular circulation of Joyce's texts that concern me here. For if the history of popular culture is understood as the history of how these troublesome distinctions between high and low have been and are constantly in the process of being made and remade, then that history should also be seen as one of the unacknowledged sites of reception for (and resistance to) Joyce's work as new publics have come to find themselves in his writing.

At first glance, this argument might seem surprising. But the very feasibility of seriously looking at Joyce's work from the vantage point of popular culture is an indication of just how far our ideas about popular culture have been revolutionized in recent years. For one thing it is no longer possible—if it ever really was—to think of popular culture as an inventory of fixed forms and practices in which, say, movies and magazines stand on one side of a divide and novels and the theater line up on the other. Nor is it plausible to gloss popular culture as the folklore of an advanced industrial society, as if it were merely the repository of our customary beliefs and traditions. Both these formulations err in painting an unduly static picture of the popular, overlooking its restless energy and ceaselessly innovative proliferation of ideas and artifacts, its constant recycling and bending of the old to newly hybrid purposes.

Giving due weight to this remarkable dynamism also tells against any implicit definition of popular culture as simply that which large numbers of people embrace and enjoy as their own. For it draws attention to the complex historical processes involved in popularization that change the terms upon which cultural texts are received and endorsed. By bringing signs and symbols into ever new configurations of discourse and meaning, popular culture effectively changes the contexts and possibilities of reading. Thus, in arguing a powerful anti-intentionalist case, Jacques Derrida has stressed that "for a writing to be writing it must continue to 'act' and to be readable even when what is called the author of the writing no longer answers for what he has written, for what he seems to have signed."

—David Glover, "A Tale of 'Unwashed Joyceans': James Joyce, Popular Culture, and Popular Theory," *Joyce and Popular Culture*, ed. R. B. Kershner (Gainesville, FL: University Press of Florida, 1996), pp. 28–29

Works by James Joyce

Chamber Music. 1907.

Dubliners. 1914.

A Portrait of the Artist as a Young Man. 1916.

Exiles: A Play in Three Acts. 1918.

Ulysses. 1922.

Pomes Penyeach. 1927.

James Clarence Mangan. 1930.

Ibsen's New Play. 1930.

Collected Poems. 1936.

Finnegans Wake. 1939.

Pastimes. 1941.

Introducing James Joyce: A Selection from Joyce's Prose. Ed.
   T. S. Eliot. 1942.

Stephen Hero: Part of the First Draft of A Portrait of the Artist
   as a Young Man. Ed. Theodore Spencer. 1944.

The Portable James Joyce. Ed. Harry Levin. 1947.

The Early Joyce: The Book Reviews 1902–03. Eds. Stanislaus
   Joyce and Ellsworth Mason. 1955.

Epiphanies. Ed. O. A. Silverman. 1956.

Letters. Ed. Stuart Gilbert and Richard Ellmann. 1957–66.
3 vols.

Critical Writings. Eds. Ellsworth Mason and Richard
Ellmann. 1959.

Scribbledehobble: The Ur-Workbook for Finnegans Wake. Ed.
Thomas Connolly. 1961.

The Cat and the Devil. 1964.

Giacomo Joyce. Ed. Richard Ellmann. 1968.

Ulysses *Notesheets in the British Museum.* Ed. Phillip F.
Herring. 1972.

Selected Letters. Ed. Richard Ellmann. 1975.

Ulysses: A Facsimile of the Manuscript. 1975. 2 vols.

A James Joyce Selection. Ed. Richard Adams. 1977.

The James Joyce Archive. Ed. Michael Groden. 1977–78.
60 vols.

James Joyce: The Index Manuscript: Finnegans Wake *Holo-
graph Workbook.* Ed. Danis Rose. 1978.

Joycechoyce: The Poems in Verse and Prose of James Joyce. Ed.
A. Norman Jeffaries and Brendan Kennelly. 1992.

Ulysses: The Dublin Edition. Ed. Danis Rose. 1997.

Works About James Joyce and *A Portrait of the Artist as a Young Man*

Adams, Robert M. *James Joyce: Common Sense and Beyond.* New York: Random House, 1967.

Anderson, Chester G., ed. *A Portrait of the Artist as a Young Man: Text, Criticism, and Notes.* New York: Viking Press, 1963.

Attridge, Derek. *The Cambridge Companion to James Joyce.* New York: Cambridge University Press, 1990.

August, Eugene R. "Father Arnall's Use of Scripture in A Portrait." *James Joyce Quarterly* 4 (1967): 275–79.

Bidwell, Bruce. *The Joycean Way: A Topographic Guide to Dubliners and A Portrait of the Artist as a Young Man.* Dublin: Wolfhound Press, 1981.

Bowen, Zack. *Musical Allusions in the Works of James Joyce.* Albany, NY: State University of New York Press, 1974.

Brandabur, Edward. *A Scrupulous Meanness.* Urbana, IL: University of Illinois Press, 1971.

Brivic, Sheldon. *Joyce Between Freud and Jung.* Port Washington, NY: Kennikat Press, 1980.

_____. *Joyce the Creator.* Madison, WI: University of Wisconsin Press, 1985.

_____. *The Veil of Signs: Joyce, Lacan, and Perception.* Urbana, IL: University of Illinois Press, 1991.

Brown, Richard. *James Joyce and Sexuality.* Cambridge: Cambridge University Press, 1985.

_____. *James Joyce.* New York: St. Martin's Press, 1992.

Cervo, Nathan. "'Seeing' as Being: The Blind Apotheosis of Stephen Dedalus." *Northern New England Review* 10 (1983): 52–65.

Cixous, Helene. *The Exile of James Joyce.* Trans. Sally A. J. Purcell. New York: David Lewis, 1972.

Collinson, Diane. "The Aesthetic Theory of Stephen Dedalus." *British Journal of Aesthetics* 23, no. 1 (1983): no pp.

Cope, Jackson I. *Joyce's Cities: Archaeologies of the Soul.* Baltimore, MD: Johns Hopkins University Press, 1981.

Cross, Richard K. *Flaubert and Joyce: The Rite of Fiction.* Princeton, NJ: Princeton University Press, 1971.

Day, Robert Adams. "How Stephen Wrote His Vampire Poem." *James Joyce Quarterly* 17 (1980): 183–97.

Ehrlich, Heyward, ed. *Light Rays: James Joyce and Modernism.* New York: New Horizon, 1984.

Ellmann, Richard. *The Consciousness of Joyce.* New York: Oxford University Press, 1977.

Foster, Thomas G. "Joyce's Grammar of Experience." *Eire-Ireland* 17, no. 4 (1982): 19–40.

Frank, Joseph. *The Widening Gyre: Crisis and Mastery in Modern Literature.* Bloomington, IL: Indiana University Press, 1963.

Froula, Christine. *Modernism's Body: Sex, Culture, and Joyce.* New York: Columbia University Press, 1996.

Givens, Seon, ed. *James Joyce: Two Decades of Criticism.* New York: Vanguard Press, 1948.

Goldman, Arnold. *The Joyce Paradox: Form and Freedom in His Fiction.* London: Routledge & Kegan Paul, 1966.

Gross, John. *James Joyce.* New York: Viking Press, 1970.

Herr, Cheryl. *Joyce's Anatomy of Culture.* Urbana, IL: University of Illinois Press, 1982.

Kenner, Hugh. *Joyce's Voices.* Berkeley, CA: University of California Press, 1978.

Kiely, Robert. *Beyond Egotism: The Fiction of James Joyce, Virginia Woolf, and D. H. Lawrence.* Cambridge: Harvard University Press, 1980.

Litz, A. Walton. *James Joyce*. New York: Twayne Publishers, 1966.

MacCabe, Colin. *James Joyce and the Revolution of the Word*. London: Macmillan, 1978.

_____, ed. *James Joyce: New Perspectives*. Bloomington, IL: Indiana University Press, 1982.

Magalaner, Marvin. *Time of Apprenticeship: The Fiction of Young James Joyce*. New York: Abelard-Shuman, 1959.

Moseley, Virginia. *Joyce and the Bible*. DeKalb, IL: Northern Illinois University Press, 1967.

Oates, Joyce Carol. "Jocoserious Joyce." *Critical Inquiry* 2 (1976): 677–88.

Paliwal, B. "The Artist as Creator in *A Portrait of the Artist as a Young Man*." *Literary Criterion* 10 (1971): 44–49.

Perelman, Bob. *The Trouble with Genius: Reading Pound, Joyce, Stein, and Zukofsky*. Berkeley, CA: University of California Press, 1994.

Reddick, Bryan. "The Importance of Tone in the Structural Rhythm of Joyce's *Portrait*." *James Joyce Quarterly* 6 (1969): 201–17.

Redford, Grant A. "The Role of Structure in Joyce's *Portrait*." *Modern Fiction Studies* 4 (1958): 21–30.

Reid, B. L. "Gnomon and Order in Joyce's *Portrait*." *Sewanee Review* 92 (1984): 397–420.

Restuccia, Frances. *Joyce and the Law of the Father*. New Haven: Yale University Press, 1989.

Rice, Thomas Jackson. *James Joyce: A Guide to Research*. New York: Garland, 1983.

Ryan, John, ed. *A Bash in the Tunnel: James Joyce by the Irish*. London: Clifton Books, 1970.

Schlossman, Beryle. *Joyce's Catholic Comedy of Language*. Madison, WI: University of Wisconsin Press, 1985.

Scott, Bonnie Kime. *Joyce and Feminism*. Bloomington, IL: Indiana University Press, 1984.

Stonehill, Brian. *The Self-Conscious Novel: Artifice in Fiction from Joyce to Pynchon*. Philadelphia: University of Pennsylvania Press, 1988.

Sucksmith, Harvey Peter. *James Joyce: A Portrait of the Artist as a Young Man*. London: Edward Arnold, 1973.

Sullivan, Kevin. *Joyce Among the Jesuits*. New York: Columbia University Press, 1957.

Tindall, William York. *James Joyce: His Way of Interpreting the Modern World*. New York: Charles Scribner's Sons, 1950.

_____. *A Reader's Guide to James Joyce*. New York: Noonday, 1965.

Zigrone, Frank. "Joyce and D'Annunzio: The Marriage of Fire and Water." *James Joyce Quarterly* 16 (1979): 253–65.

Index of
Themes and Ideas